THE PRODUCTIVE ONLINE AND OFFLINE PROFESSOR

OTHER BOOKS IN THE THRIVE ONLINE SERIES

Thrive Online: A New Approach to Building Expertise and Confidence as an Online Educator

By Shannon Riggs

Series Foreword by Kathryn E. Linder

Foreword by Penny Ralston-Berg

THE PRODUCTIVE
and Offline
ONLINE PROFESSOR
A Practical Guide

Bonni Stachowiak

SERIES FOREWORD BY KATHRYN E. LINDER
FOREWORD BY ROBERT TALBERT

Sty/us

STERLING, VIRGINIA

Published by Stylus Publishing, LLC.
22883 Quicksilver Drive
Sterling, Virginia 20166-2019

Library of Congress Cataloging-in-Publication Data
Names: Stachowiak, Bonni Jean, 1971- author.
Title: The productive online and offline professor : a practical guide / Bonni Stachowiak ; Series foreword by Kathryn E. Linder ; Foreword by Robert Talbert.
Description: First edition. | Sterling, Virginia : Stylus Publishing, [2020] | Series: Thrive online series | Includes bibliographical references and index. | Summary: "The Productive Online Professor assists those who teach online and blended courses with managing their personal productivity. Faculty are often expected to provide support and feedback to learners outside of normal work hours in non-traditional classes. Programs that are designed with more asynchronous content may cause faculty to perceive that it is difficult to ever press the "off button"on their teaching.The author offers guidance and suggests software tools for streamlining communication and productivity that enable faculty to better balance their lives while giving rich feedback to students. Part 1 addresses the challenges in defining productivity and presents a working definition for the text. Part 2 describes the ability to communicate using both synchronous and asynchronous methods, along with ways of enriching such communication. Part 3 describes methods for finding, curating, and sharing relevant knowledge both within one's courses and to a broader personal learning network (PLN). Part 4 examines specific tools for navigating the unique challenges of productivity while teaching online. It includes ways to grade

more productively while still providing rich feedback to students. Part 5 shares techniques for keeping one's course materials current and relevant in the most efficient ways possible. The Productive Online Professor is a practical guide for how to provide high quality online classes to diverse students. This book shares specific technology and other tools that may be used in charting a course toward greater productivity. It is intended to be a professional resource for fulfilling our roles with excellence and joy, while managing other priorities in our personal and professional lives"– Provided by publisher.

Identifiers: LCCN 2019049298 (print) | LCCN 2019049299 (ebook) | ISBN   9781620367292 (hardcover) | ISBN 9781620367308 (paperback) | ISBN   9781620367315 (pdf) | ISBN 9781620367322 (ebook)
Subjects: LCSH: Education, Higher--Web-based instruction. | Distance   education--Computer-assisted instruction. | College teachers--Time   management. | Educational technology. | Communication in higher education.
Classification: LCC LB2395.7 .S763 2020 (print) | LCC LB2395.7 (ebook) | DDC 378.1/7344678--dc23
LC record available at https://lccn.loc.gov/2019049298
LC ebook record available at https://lccn.loc.gov/2019049299

13-digit ISBN: 978-1-62036-729-2 (cloth)
13-digit ISBN: 978-1-62036-730-8 (paperback)
13-digit ISBN: 978-1-62036-731-5 (library networkable e-edition)
13-digit ISBN: 978-1-62036-732-2 (consumer e-edition)

Printed in the United States of America

All first editions printed on acid-free paper that meets the American National Standards Institute Z39-48 Standard.

Bulk Purchases

Quantity discounts are available for use in workshops and for staff development.
Call 1-800-232-0223

First Edition, 2020

To our two children, Luke and Hannah, who make me want to be more fully present in life and not miss a bit of all the good stuff that is right in front of me.

CONTENTS

SERIES FOREWORD

Welcome to another addition to the Thrive Online series, a collection of books designed to focus on the needs, interests, and best practices of instructors teaching online with the ultimate goal of better serving online students.

In *The Productive Online and Offline Professor*, Bonni Stachowiak shares practical steps for how to incorporate the tools and strategies that enhance productivity. One of my favorite parts of this book is how Stachowiak focuses on not only the *what* and *how* of being a more productive higher education professional but also the *why*. She argues for prioritizing the concept of and creating systems for efficiency so we can focus on the central goal of higher education: improving the experiences of our students.

Stachowiak's own experiences as an instructor, an administrator, and a podcaster (she hosts *Teaching in Higher Ed* each week) make her the perfect mentor for readers looking to increase their productivity through small, manageable steps that can be incorporated immediately.

I asked Stachowiak to contribute to this series because of her passion for improving the lives of her students and her peers in higher education. She has not only a vast knowledge of what works to help students learn but also a commitment to constantly looking for efficient ways to create transformative learning experiences in a range of classroom modalities.

Stachowiak has tested how to incorporate a range of productivity strategies into the day-to-day lives of academics and higher education professionals. She is the first person I turn to when I have questions about what new app I should be checking out, or what new teaching tool I should consider. She is selfless in her efforts to positively impact the lives of her students and colleagues through sharing her productivity strategies and tips.

In adding this book to the Thrive Online series, I am excited to contribute to the ongoing conversation about how we can be more meaningfully productive in our higher education careers. Like all of the contributors to the Thrive Online series, Stachowiak is a fearless, committed thought leader who has embraced how technology can enhance our professional work and teaching experiences.

I hope you will join the conversation using #ThriveOnline to share your own experiences in the online teaching and learning landscape as we continue to grow the community of committed and passionate online learning advocates in higher education. Come thrive with us!

Kathryn E. Linder
Series Editor
July 2019

FOREWORD

Everything about higher education is based on trust. Students trust professors to be knowledgeable in their disciplines, grade fairly, and be willing and able to help. Professors trust students to work hard, give their best efforts, and turn in honest work. Administrators trust faculty to work toward the vision and goals that they lay out, and faculty trust administrators to lead the institution down the right paths. This web of trust is all-encompassing, and without it higher education becomes fundamentally dysfunctional.

At the most basic level, the web of trust is made up of *people*—people who work from a position of relaxed control over their time and tasks, so that they have the capacity to know exactly what task or person requires their skill and full attention at any given time. Put differently, professors' trustworthiness is proportional to the amount of control they have over their work. This is especially clear if that control is lacking. Suppose you email a colleague whose inbox contains hundreds, even thousands, of unprocessed emails. Can you fully trust that you'll get a response that's timely or has the correct information? Suppose a student emails an adviser to set up a meeting, but the adviser is also inundated with email and isn't good with managing a busy calendar. Can that student trust that the meeting will take place, or that the adviser will be "all there" even if the meeting occurs?

Early in my career as a faculty member, I had an encounter with a dean who brought this trust-presence-control connection to life. As I was walking down the hall he stopped me and asked, "So, I'll see you at 2:00 today?" I froze—I had no idea what he was talking about. Recovering, I lamely said, "Sure, see you then," then marched right back to my office to hunt for the meeting request in my email. It was buried in my inbox, which had amassed hundreds of emails dating back two years. Although I had scanned the email subject, I hadn't put the meeting on the calendar, apparently saving that task for later. That search diverted 30 minutes of time that could have been spent on any number of tasks that I constantly complained I had no time to do. But it could have been worse: I might not have run into the dean at all. In that case, I would have missed the meeting or shown up late only after he had waited and then had his assistant call to remind me. I would have committed the cardinal sin of higher education: wasting another person's time.

Although I had worked for years to build a reputation as a strong contributor at that college, it could have all been undone by one missed email that led to one missed meeting that led to the dean labeling me, fairly or otherwise, as not fully trustworthy. *Education is based on trust, which is based on being fully present, which is grounded in control over our work*.

This book, by my friend Bonni Stachowiak, is a splendid, useful guide for all of us in higher education—especially but not exclusively those who teach online—for getting our acts together and gaining control over our work, thus making us fully present and fully trustworthy. In it you'll encounter many big ideas, such as the Getting Things Done, or "GTD," system of productivity, whose importance for educators cannot be overstated. But part of the genius of this book is that the big ideas are broken down into simple, practical, incremental steps that anyone can take, *today*. (If you are one of those people with hundreds or thousands of emails in your inbox and despair of ever regaining control, you are in for a game-changing experience.) Then, you can use the book as a field manual—perhaps using some of the numerous digital and analog tools for productivity that the book details—to make those small steps habitual and aggregate more good habits as you journey toward being a truly productive, fully present professor.

Through her *Teaching in Higher Ed* podcast and now in this book, Bonni Stachowiak has shown she understands two complementary truths about being a faculty member: Our work is vital, and there is much more to life than work. She understands that the purpose of productivity is not merely to *do more work* but rather to achieve an end: having the freedom necessary to focus fully on what matters the most to us. This book is her gift to the rest of us: a practical user's guide that lays out a clear, compelling pathway toward a vision of faculty work that is realistic and attainable even (perhaps especially) for those who are so overwhelmed that they do not know where or how to begin. I am confident that this book will help you transform the way you do your work so that you are fully present and trustworthy.

Robert Talbert, PhD
Professor of Mathematics
Grand Valley State University
Allendale, Michigan, USA

ACKNOWLEDGMENTS

Thank you to Kathryn E. Linder for inviting me to be a part of the Thrive Online book series. In addition to getting to collaborate with someone I admire greatly, I have been able to get to know her even better and consider her a mentor and a friend.

To my students, who have helped shape my approaches tremendously and brought me such joy, thank you. You help me discern what is most important in life and make me a better teacher, learner, and mentor.

Thanks to my mom, who has always been a tremendous encouragement to me. She is also a superb writer and editor. Isabeau Iqbal also helped me see some of the unexpected ways that people might find value in *The Productive Online and Offline Professor*.

My deepest appreciation goes out to each of you who reviewed or edited the book and gave me feedback on how to make it even better. The Teaching in Higher Ed Slack group provided me with plenty of questions related to productivity since we first established the community. Annemarie Perez was especially helpful in sharing her experiences getting started with setting up a system, and Linda Oakleaf always provides me with such encouragement. My colleagues at Vanguard University (especially Sandie Morgan and Julie Wilson) helped shape this book through their insightful questions in recent years, as well as through their support. I am thankful for the opportunity to dream a million dreams with Shannon Jonsson and continually find ways to use productivity approaches to better serve our faculty and students.

Harold Jarche has been a constant source of wisdom on personal knowledge mastery. Other guests on the *Teaching in Higher Ed* podcast who spoke about personal knowledge management (PKM) have also been instrumental in helping me articulate that portion of the book. My gratitude extends to Crystal Renfro for agreeing to join Mary Axford all the way back on episode 9 to talk about PKM. Sadly, Mary passed away about a year after we recorded. I appreciate Crystal sharing some slices of her grief with me, as she continues to miss her collaborator and friend.

There have also been many contributions from podcast guests who spoke about productivity. Natalie Houston has been an inspiration regarding her ability to get us thinking about living a life with more ease. Robert Talbert has been on the show several times, too, to share how he manages such a full life with integrity and concern for his students.

The writers of the *ProfHacker* blog continually provide tangible ways for us all to enhance our teaching, tech, and productivity. I am ever grateful for those who contribute to *Hybrid Pedagogy*. You keep me thinking about the ways I use technology in my teaching, always having my students at the center. Special thanks to Jesse Stommel,

Sean Michael Morris, and Maha Bali for challenging me to think more critically in all my creative endeavors and teaching.

I am especially grateful to my best friend and partner, Dave Stachowiak. You embrace the same principles I do about what it means to be productive and how we can *show up* more for our lives when we improve our approaches. Thank you for being a wonderful collaborator, encourager, spouse, and parent to our children.

INTRODUCTION

What does it mean to be productive in our roles as professors? What would it look like to have more peace in our lives and not find ourselves constantly in reaction mode, to know that we were investing our time in ways that were most meaningful to us? How would our lives be different if we knew that all our commitments were recorded, that there was not a chance a single task was going to be forgotten, that not one piece of follow-up from our classes would fall through the cracks?

What if our students knew we were committed to serving their needs? If they were confident that they were going to be regularly presented with relevant, engaging, and current resources to heighten their learning and hear back from us when they have questions?

That is what this book has been designed to accomplish. *The Productive Online and Offline Professor* was conceptualized to serve those who teach fully online or blended courses. However, the guidance provided is broad enough to apply to anyone who teaches in a higher education context.

This book helps us aim for improved productivity, but not so that we can have ever-higher head counts in our classes or achieve more exceptional results according to others' measures. The approaches described in this text provide ways to streamline those aspects of our work that allow for improved productivity without lessening our ability to have authentic connections with our students. We make what we can more efficient so we can be more fully present in our teaching and other parts of our lives.

One of the hardest parts of writing about productivity is overcoming the following perceptions that many in academic circles have regarding this topic: speeding up our work can translate into reducing the personal attention we pay to our students, the work of teaching can be seen as easily replaced or robotic, or boosting our workflow efficiencies might mean missing out on some of the more creative aspects of our vocation.

The resistance toward thinking of ourselves as productive workers is not new (Tierney, 1999). We dislike being referred to in ways that mechanize our work, yet we strive for achievement and want to fulfill the commitments we make to those who depend on us in our increasingly interdependent work. Administrative leaders who focus on "scaling" online learning often leave the human elements of teaching and learning too far removed from the discussion. We want meaningful, significant, complex connections with our online students, and no new set of macros is going to make that possible.

Middaugh (2001) reminds us that "productivity cannot be measured until the nature of the work being assessed

The approaches described in this text provide ways to streamline aspects of our work that allow for improved productivity without lessening our ability to have authentic connections with our students.

#ThriveOnline

is well defined" (p. 8). How much time we are expected to spend teaching versus devoting our efforts toward research will undoubtedly shape how we measure our effectiveness. The priorities of a professor at a research institution are likely to look considerably different from those of a professor at a community college, where research requirements are often minimal.

The pursuit of productivity can extend well beyond our professional endeavors. Meyer's (2012) research reveals that those of us who teach online often pursued this type of work because of its scheduling flexibility. We might have small children at home or family members with health challenges. As our lives have reached a point where we need more flexibility in our teaching, we are often in need of tools to help us navigate our work and the balance between the personal and the professional.

When we teach online, some of our efforts can go unnoticed. Gauging our results is difficult. Our productivity and effectiveness may be reduced to student head counts and course evaluations. As illustrated by Middaugh (2001), the attempts to measure faculty members' productivity are likely to focus far more on inputs (what we do) than outputs (the results achieved).

As online instructors, we are often expected to provide support and feedback to learners outside of regular work hours. Programs or courses that are designed with greater emphasis on asynchronous content can make it difficult for us to press the "off button" on our teaching. The need for methods to have improved productivity in our lives often extends well beyond the instruction environment.

As we consider ways to enhance our productivity, it is paramount to know what is most important to us. Are we aiming to have more time to invest in mentoring our students, or do we want the ability to pursue additional grant opportunities? Are we seeking to experience less stress through having a better handle on our projects and tasks, or is it more important that we focus on our integrity in being people who do what we say we will do?

For several years, I have hosted a podcast called *Teaching in Higher Ed* that has two foci: teaching and personal productivity. Concerning the second aim of the podcast, the following words are included in the introduction to each episode: "We also share ways we can improve our productivity so we can have more peace in our lives and be even more present for our students." Being fully present is a challenging aim. Those who can live in the moment experience less stress and are more able to appreciate what is before them. I struggle to be present, often preferring to focus on the future in my own personal and professional endeavors. While being able to consider what is possible down the road is a valuable skill, so is being engaged in the moment that is now:

> There is one thing we can do, and the happiest people are those who can do it to the limit of their ability. We can be completely present. We can be all here. We can give . . . our attention to the opportunity before us. (Mark Van Doren as cited in Allen, 2015, p. 3)

When I am at my most productive, I avoid fretting about what is falling through the cracks. I do not have to wonder if I am working toward meaningful goals. My students know that they have my full attention when I am with them, whether in a videoconference class session or a one-on-one phone conversation. My husband and our children also know that when I am with them they have my focus. *The Productive Online and Offline Professor* aims to describe how I am able to do that and share others' approaches as well.

Being present for our students (online or face-to-face) is vital to our effectiveness as educators. In a study on quality online education, a participant emphasized the need for presence by stating,

> You really have to rewire your thinking about how you manage your time . . . and your presence. . . . [You're] not there with students, so how do you make that happen?
>
> I don't know if it's time management so much as it is a presence management issue. (Whalen, 2009, p. iv)

In a study conducted by Bruner (2007), faculty members estimated that it takes twice as long to develop an online course as it does an in-person one. The frequent use of asynchronous communication tools in an online course, such as email, can often lead to more time being required to address students' needs adequately.

The Productive Online and Offline Professor aims to identify fulcrum points in our work, such that we can have more time to invest in more meaningful interactions with our students. As we streamline our communication, our

When I am at my most productive, I avoid fretting about what is falling through the cracks.

#ThriveOnline

students can have a better idea of how to achieve their academic goals and we can spend less time clarifying aspects of the course that have already been articulated. As we locate, curate, and share knowledge, the examples we use in our online courses can be more current and relevant for our students. As we use tools that help us simplify and automate parts of our work, we can have that much more time for the unexpected events that inevitably come up during a course. Finally, as we strive to keep online courses as current and as relevant as possible, we can spend less time updating information and more time investing in our students.

This book presents approaches to achieve greater productivity in an academic context. Many of the examples are specifically geared toward those who teach online. However, this book is pertinent to all who instruct in higher education, facilitating online, blended, or face-to-face courses.

This book is intended to be a practical guide for fulfilling our roles with excellence and joy while managing other priorities in our personal and professional lives. Note that the word in the previous sentence is *excellence*, not *perfection*. Brown (2012) has regularly worked to free us from the guilt we feel when we do not live up to our own and others' expectations and are trapped in our attempts to be perfect. She states, "We risk missing out on joy when we get too busy chasing down the extraordinary" (p. 125). This book aims to reduce the friction in the way we approach our work, yet recognizes we have individual differences in what will work best.

This book is pertinent to all who instruct in higher education, facilitating online, blended, or face-to-face courses.

#ThriveOnline

Each part of *The Productive Online and Offline Professor* is devoted to productivity on your terms, according to your priorities and preferences:

- Part One addresses the challenges in translating intention into action and proposes methods for setting and accomplishing goals.
- Part Two describes the ability to communicate using both synchronous and asynchronous methods, along with ways of enriching such communication.
- Part Three prescribes techniques for finding, curating, and sharing relevant knowledge both to students within one's courses and to a broader personal learning network (PLN).
- Part Four examines specific tools for navigating the unique challenges of productivity while teaching online. It includes ways to grade more productively, which in this case means providing rich feedback to students while not wasting time on the aspects of grading that do not align with that aim.
- Part Five shares techniques for keeping one's course materials current and relevant in the most efficient ways possible.

Located at thriveonlineseries.com, an online supplement ensures that the tools mentioned are kept updated with any changes that come after the publication date. Visit that site often to keep the inspiration going from the book, as well as to discover other tools that were not included in the book. The website also provides updated links to all the applications, services, and tools. Another way to leverage greater benefits from reading *The Productive Online and Offline Professor* (as well as the other books in the Thrive Online series) is to engage in community with others.

The hashtag #ThriveOnline is used throughout the book to extend invitations to share reflections, ideas, and recommendations. Hashtags are used on Twitter and other social media as a means for grouping conversations and making it easy to see what is happening within a given topic. A search for #ThriveOnline will show recent discussions that are occurring about the books within the series. What are the challenges that get in the way of achieving greater productivity in your teaching and in the other parts of your life? Pursuing enhanced productivity is not a solo journey. The #ThriveOnline conversation will help build community and remind us all that we are not alone in these efforts.

PURSUING PRODUCTIVITY

What are the aims of increased productivity when teaching online (or offline)? This section introduces the critiques made for gauging faculty members' productivity and articulates what is possible with greater efficiency and effectiveness in online teaching.

Ultimately, the goal of being productive while teaching online is to be present for our students, effectively facilitate learning while establishing systems that allow us to fulfill our commitments, and have greater peace in our lives. Focusing on being more efficient in our teaching does not mean we have to deemphasize effective pedagogy or care any less for our students.

We need to be careful not to overemphasize making things faster if we are pursuing unproductive or unhealthy aims. The authors of *The Slow Professor* (Berg & Seeber, 2016) criticize the so-called culture of speed that is so prevalent in higher education. They are critical of the corporatization of colleges and universities, and the "distractedness and fragmentation [that] characterize[s] contemporary academic life" (p. 90). Institutions' financial challenges can quickly be translated into so-called solutions of implementing larger class sizes, asking faculty to perform administrative tasks outside the scope of their functional roles, and increasing the use of the contingent workforce.

Berg and Seeber (2016) offer some relief to tenured professors in *The Slow Professor*, reminding us of the importance of reflection and stillness in our work. However, there are criticisms regarding how their guidance might apply to those who are a part of the contingent academic workforce. Adjunct faculty increasingly share their stories of taking on more than a full-time workload, an attempt to cobble together enough income to pay the bills. Does the higher education contingent workforce have the luxury of focusing on slowing down?

Mitch Tropin works as an adjunct and coordinates his commute times between six institutions in and around Washington DC. He reveals, "You never know when a class will be canceled or a full-time professor will bump you at the last minute" (Fredrickson, 2015, para. 9).

THE ROLE OF THE ONLINE PROFESSOR

The role of a professor looks drastically different depending on the institution as well as the various types of students being served. Teaching online only adds to that complexity. The tools used to teach the courses can vary from those of face-to-face classes at some institutions. The marketing messages used to solicit students for online programs emphasize flexibility and regular opportunities to engage with the faculty teaching the courses. Unless different expectations are set, it can be made to seem like a professor will be available at all hours of the day and night to support learners in online programs.

Our work as online professors may include the following types of responsibilities:

- Teaching (online or hybrid courses)
- Research
- University service
- Meetings
- Publishing
- Conferences

Many online professors teach as adjuncts and hold other jobs. Beyond our professional duties, we may have significant others, children, parents, and other family members who require care, as well as organizations we belong to outside of work. There is a lot to navigate.

Regardless of what we are aiming toward in the desire to improve our productivity, some practices can help us reflect on what is most important to us, eradicate unrecognized time wasters, and ultimately be more present for those we teach. The following section explores various understandings of productivity. It also articulates fundamental principles that will be true regardless of what technique is being implemented.

PRODUCTIVITY: A DEFINITION

Being productive is not about being able to accomplish tasks faster if that means detracting from our abilitites to be present in our teaching and other aspects of our lives. However, if we can automate tasks that will hinder our ability to focus on those we serve, then that type of efficiency is worth pursuing.

Faculty productivity is sadly most often translated into how much research gets conducted. Although the techniques in this book could be used to pursue larger research portfolios, focusing myopically on that one aspect of productivity would be an incredibly short-sighted way of gauging faculty productivity at large. The sole measure lacks the appreciation for how diverse our institutions are and the focus on teaching that is present at many universities and colleges.

Productivity is being aware of our commitments and being able to prioritize them holistically. Productivity allows us to have more peace in our lives because we are far less likely to allow things to fall through the cracks. Productivity is about reducing the friction in our systems such that we have more capability for attending to the people we care most about. Houston (2015) shared her definition of *productivity* on the *Teaching in Higher Ed* podcast: "Productivity, to me, is not about doing more things faster. It is about doing the things that are most important to me and creating the kind of life I want to have" (para. 1). We are at our most productive when we can leverage our strengths in our work. When we have established systems for recording, organizing, and reflecting on our priorities, our minds are freed up for more creative endeavors.

There are three aspects to this definition of *productivity*:

1. *Awareness of commitments and priorities*: There can be a temptation to think that we can keep track of all the things that need to be done in our lives in our heads. However, if we think just about the number of emails most of us get in a single day that contain some kind of request from someone else, we can see that relying on our memory is not enough. Productive online professors know what they have committed to accomplish and what their priorities are at any given time.

2. *Enough margin to meet emerging needs*: Because the overwhelming majority of online students pursue that venue for at least some portion of their coursework because of its inherent flexibility, it is essential that we be prepared to respond to them quickly and support them in their learning. There are also times when we hear about an upcoming deadline for a conference presentations proposal just before the due date. Having the capacity to take on additional tasks as they emerge can help us avoid missing out on exciting

opportunities, as well as best serve our students. Productive online professors have enough room in their lives to attend to learners' needs as they become aware of them and to capitalize on last-minute serendipitous occurrences.

3. *Established systems and approaches to help maximize investment of time*: If a task can be made easier through some kind of automation or workflow, it makes sense to leverage the possibilities. The only exception to this principle is when considering our relationships with other people. Human connections should not be made more efficient. However, having systems that help us work smarter can free up more time for engaging in those essential relationships. Productive online professors develop approaches to ease aspects of their work that can save them time, to free them up to have more authentic connections with their students and colleagues.

As productive online professors we are aware of our commitments, invest our time in making meaningful connections with our students, and regularly seek to develop our students' learning. We have adequate space in our lives to pursue unplanned things that come our way.

FUNDAMENTAL PRINCIPLES

More than 100 tactics are described in this book for how to improve one's productivity. That does not mean that each one should be implemented in a person's life, however. When reading a book that offers prescriptions for how to be more productive, it is easy to become overwhelmed or fail to leverage as much as one hopes.

People's productivity systems must work for them, in the short and long term. *The Productive Online and Offline Professor* is not intended to be followed like a recipe, step-by-step, regardless of what ingredients are on hand or what one's preferences are. Instead, each of the book's five parts concludes with a "Take Action" section, where one or two approaches may be identified as most relevant and ripe for experimentation.

One cautionary note is vital in learning more about productivity: Avoid the temptation to be perfectionistic about your productivity practices. I regularly have weeks when I consider myself to have been "productive" and others where I lacked that feeling of accomplishment. This is not a game of crossing the finish line, but rather aligning ourselves with practices that help us fulfill our commitments and be present for others. Robinson (2012) exemplifies this quest for showing more vulnerability and not allowing guilt to take over when we miss the mark. She reminds us, "Productivity practices are predicated on grappling with constant scarcity. Not enough time. Not enough control. Not enough perspective. Not organized enough. Not reliable enough. Not [fill in the blank] enough" (para. 7). Robinson is working toward the constant awareness that she is enough even when not enough actions were checked off on her task list during a given week.

While we are not aiming for perfection, two fundamental principles are reflected throughout this book: building trustworthy productivity systems and being worthy of trust. By focusing on principles over practices, we can ground ourselves in what is most important and not get caught up in the minutiae of thinking we just have not found the right trick yet. Regardless of how we decide to organize our virtual files, or whether we use a paper or a digital calendar, the following principles will support a sustainable productivity system and are foundational to the pursuit of productivity.

Building Trustworthy Productivity Systems

Our productivity practices can sometimes get us into trouble. The challenge is that we cannot trust them. We want them to show us what is most important and to be able to rely on them to track our commitments. Instead, we can find ourselves having to work around the systems that we set up because we know that the information we have fed into them is not accurate, or at least not as precise as needed. We want our minds to be cleared after engaging with our productivity systems. All too often, though, we wind up feeling even more overwhelmed and unclear on where to focus our attention. As Dini (2014) argues,

> To rely on our systems, we need to be able to trust them. When we trust our environments to support us, to not be intrusive, to engage us when it would be best, we can use them to develop what we find to be meaningful (p. 36).

Most of us have built productivity systems that regularly misinform us about where things stand, or what requires our attention. One example of this is with deadlines. In task management systems (to-do lists), there is a place to establish a deadline for any action. Instead of thinking about whether an actual date exists by which a particular task must be completed, we enter into wishful thinking. We might say to ourselves, "It would be good to get it done by Friday, for the committee to have a few weeks to think about it before the next time we are together in person." Monday would work just as well to circulate the information to the committee members, or even the following Friday. After all, the next committee meeting is not scheduled until three weeks from now.

We start setting arbitrary, meaningless deadlines for all our tasks. Before we know it, we have established a system of tracking tasks that is not trustworthy. The tool we use to track all of our tasks tells us that tasks are due by a given date when in fact we just wish we would finish them by that time. As the situation snowballs, most of our tasks appear to be overdue and therefore in need of immediate attention when in fact many of the deadlines were merely the result of wishful thinking.

Being Worthy of Trust

By having reliable productivity systems, we have an opportunity to be worthy of others' trust. Can we fulfill our commitments to others? Do we do what we say we will do? Are we the type of people who are continually seeking to become more knowledgeable and skilled in our chosen vocation?

Stephen Covey (2004, 2009, 2012) defined *trust* in many of his books as having two components: character and competence. Others come to trust us because we fulfill our commitments, tell the truth, and are other-centered. Trust extends beyond having good character, however.

Trust is also built by being good at what we do, by being competent. We become trusted online professors because we are capable teachers and are regularly seeking to become even more effective at facilitating learning. Our quest to remain up to date and relevant in our disciplines never ceases, yet we also trust that our students bring valuable insights into their learning experiences and have much to offer the learning community and us.

One of the principles articulated throughout *The Productive Online and Offline Professor* is that following through on what we commit to matters. Our students are counting on us to model this value for them, as are our faculty colleagues. This book helps us realize that aim.

USE WHAT WORKS: ANALOG VERSUS DIGITAL

Some people gravitate toward paper-based aids, whereas others instead find a technological way to set up their systems. My advice is to use what works, in terms of both your personal preferences and the approaches that will produce the least amount of friction. These contrasting ways of working are often referred to as analog versus digital tools.

As I type these words, there are sticky notes adhered to my monitor and desk hutch. As I identified each suggested change made by the publisher, I created a separate physical note to keep me focused. I certainly could have placed those notes in digital format and virtually checked each item off as I finished. However, there is something incredibly motivating about seeing the amount of work remaining in this particular revision stage become smaller and smaller as I crumple up each note. Seeing the brightly colored paper in my peripheral vision provides me with the ability to resist the temptation to shift my attention to an activity more exciting than this part of the writing process.

In contrast, I have not found it helpful to track general to-do items with sticky notes. In fact, it may even be unhelpful. These small pieces of paper are too easy for me to misplace and they often are not with me when I am trying to move a project forward. I have an office at my university, as well as a dedicated work spot at home. There is also a coffee shop down the hill from our house that occasionally serves as a place to get things done. I need to have the tools I need for my productivity system with me at all times, which is why digital tools are often my preference. However, there are times when an analog approach rules supreme.

Another aspect of using what works is to consider the primary function of an application. Occasionally, podcast listeners will email me and inquire as to why I recommended a particular product on the show. Recently, a professor asked why I did not suggest Google Keep (a virtual notebook app) when I was sharing about social bookmarking tools. My response was that Google Keep can serve the purpose of saving bookmarks, but the social bookmarking services that I recommended all had extended features to more effectively share categories of information with others than Google Keep.

It all depends on the primary ways we want to leverage a given application. I try to keep the number of different services I use to a minimum. This helps my ongoing learning about various services result in extending the value of the tools. But if I minimize my applications too much, I will miss out on the unique challenges that the developers have attempted to solve in the creation of their service. I provide more recommendations specific to the choice of analog versus digital in Part One.

GETTING STARTED

Beginning to think more about productivity and where to start can feel overwhelming. It is not necessary to read *The Productive Online and Offline Professor* in order from start to finish. However, I do recommend starting with Part One, which, along with this introduction, lays a solid foundation regarding terminology and fundamental approaches. Then, feel free to navigate to the parts that are most relevant to what you are trying to accomplish, in terms of becoming more productive.

It will help you truly adopt what you are reading if you pause along the way and identify steps you want to take to improve your systems. The "Take Action" section at the end of each part provides ideas for things you can tackle to translate theory into action. Consider not reading the whole book at once, which will make it easier for you to put the information into practice.

These are some areas you may consider focusing on as you make your learning tangible:

- Review the fundamental principles described in the introduction and determine whether any changes would help you with your productivity.
- Regularly reflect on the ways that designing or improving your systems will help you achieve your goals—which will keep you motivated along the way.
- Set goals using one of the three methods described in Part One.
- Determine one method to use in an upcoming class to facilitate communication with your students more effectively based on the advice from Part Two.
- Establish a personal knowledge management (PKM) system using the approaches shared in Part Three.
- Identify one workflow that can be improved using checklists, workflows, or automation as described in Part Four.
- Start using a password manager or audit your back-up method(s) as prescribed in Part Five to avoid serious productivity deficiencies that can arise when passwords are hacked, hard drives fail, or identities are stolen.

The trouble with feeling overwhelmed is that it can prevent us from taking any action at all. The best way to become more productive is to start somewhere. If you find yourself having difficulty determining what steps to take, consult the Take Action steps outlined at the end of each part and pick just one step to begin traveling down the path of translating your intention into action.

TAKE ACTION: INTRODUCTION

This is an opportunity to reflect on which steps are most important to take after reading through the introduction. Here are specific next actions you may want to consider and record your thoughts about to increase the impact of the book:

❏ Determine where to store actions to take as you read this book. Capture one to three steps to take from having read the introduction. In Parts One through Five, the Take Action section will always have some ideas to get you started.

❏ Spend some time reflecting on the meaning and purpose of productivity. If you can achieve "maximum" productivity, what will that free you from and what will you be able to focus more on?

❏ Visit teachinginhighered.com/episodes and view the category of episodes about productivity. Listen to the two episodes that are most related to areas where you feel your productivity is being challenged. Instead of listening online, you can search for *Teaching in Higher Ed* on whatever podcast app you have on your smartphone (Apple Podcasts, Google Podcasts, TuneIn, or via Stitcher Radio). Identify what resonated most with you as you listened and what specific steps you can take to implement one thing from each episode.

PART ONE

TRANSLATING INTENTION INTO ACTION

TRANSLATING INTENTION INTO ACTION

As articulated in the introduction, productive professors are aware of their commitments and priorities and have systems and approaches to help maximize their investment of time. We therefore want to be freed up to have enough margin to meet the needs that emerge in the moment. All of this is about translating our intentions into the actions that we can take to reach our goals and live out our values.

I begin this part of *The Productive Online and Offline Professor* by exploring the practice of goal setting. I examine why so many of us fail to achieve what we hoped and provide a few different ways of determining and articulating our goals.

Next, I present an extensive look at a practice called Getting Things Done (GTD). Examples are included that are most relevant to how to turn our intentions into reality within a higher education context. I share about the importance of stepping back, reflecting, and ensuring that things do not fall between the cracks using a process of weekly and monthly reviews.

Finally, I consider the engine that drives a lot of the process of accomplishing our goals: the task manager. I remember when I was in college my mom would suggest writing a list of the things that were stressing me out. I could then prioritize tasks and develop a plan of attack. Today's task manager approaches can be as simple as that or quite intricate. Regardless of approach, having an inventory of what needs to be done is an essential part of any productive professor's tool kit.

GOAL SETTING

In the introduction, we looked at the various roles we perform as online instructors, such as teaching, research, publishing, and conferences. While the percentage of time we invest in any of these areas can vary widely, the need to establish our own framework for success is essential. We may want to redesign a course or move a series of classes online, obtain a full-time faculty position, publish a journal article in our discipline, present at a conference, or write a book.

The subject of goal setting is likely to either energize or exhaust a person. We must consider where we are headed, or we will likely not make progress toward those things we find most important. However, when unexpected events occur in our lives that prevent us from accomplishing our aims, goal setting can hardly seem like a beneficial exercise.

Especially grueling approaches are New Year's resolutions or annual goal setting. By the time nine months have gone by, circumstances are often entirely different from when we first began the goal-setting process. It is easy to become disillusioned about the process of goal setting when we are unable to see that we made meaningful progress toward those outcomes we considered to be most important to us when the planning process began.

Instead of reflecting on *what we want to accomplish* in our goal-setting processes, Natalie Houston (2014) posits a focus on *who we want to be* this year. She advises thinking of the various roles that we play (e.g., parent, friend, or partner) or areas that are important to us (e.g., learning, activism, or environmentalism). Her method involves coming up with a one- to two-sentence description of "who you want to be in each role . . . (for instance: 'I am a loving and thoughtful spouse')" (para. 4). Alternatively, Houston (2014) proposes that we identify three words that "answer the question of who you want to be more holistically, regarding key qualities you want to embody or actions you want to take that cut across the different roles of your life" (para. 5).

Allen (2015) suggests that we think about goals in relation to various horizons (or levels). There are current actions, which need to be accomplished but may or may not be aligned with a particular project. Allen defines any desired outcome that will take more than one action (or step) to accomplish as a *project*. Those projects fall under different areas of responsibility or roles we take on in achieving our broader goals. He also proposes considering one-year and two-year goals, as well as goals that stretch to three to five years. Finally, Allen recommends considering those goals that we aim to complete within our lifetime.

Instead of starting with long-term goals (the lifetime goals), he inverts his goal-setting model. He asserts that when the smaller tasks are out of control, attempting to bring about a broader perspective can be too much of a challenge. Once the foundational systems are in place for managing the day-to-day tasks, Allen (2015) suggests that it is that much easier to tackle the more complex thinking and reflecting required from a bigger perspective.

Critiques of the Classic Advice

Management training on goal setting often starts with the overly familiar acronym to describe specific, measurable, achievable, relevant, and time-based goals, or SMART goals. There are plenty of variations on the acronym, but the ubiquity of it remains.

The difficulty in relying on SMART goals to help navigate the process is that none of the words that make up the acronym facilitate getting closer to determining whether or not the target is worthy of pursuit. Dick Grote (2017) illustrates this in *Harvard Business Review*:

> The stale SMART acronym can be a major obstacle to goal-setting success, and too often, it's the only support that is offered to those charged with setting goals. While the SMART test may be a useful minor mechanism for making sure that a goal statement has been phrased properly (in the same way that a spell-checker is a useful mechanism for flagging any misspelled words in a document), it

provides no help in determining whether the goal itself is a good idea. In other words, a goal can easily be SMART without being wise.

Grote (2017) does indicate that the SMART acronym can assist in identifying goals that are poorly articulated. Goals should be written so that others can discern the results they are intended to achieve. A completion date helps drive progress toward the aim. Specifying milestones to demonstrate progress toward the goal can prevent the pervasive challenge of procrastination.

Locke and Latham (2002), however, spent 35 years studying the practice of making goals realistic and question its efficacy in their 2019 article. When goals are made to be realistic, the authors argue, they all too often lack the difficulty required to encourage the goal setter to produce the most significant effort toward the goal. Instead of admonishing ourselves to do our best in working toward our goals we are far better off to have had challenging goals in the first place and to put forth the effort it will take to achieve the performance we seek.

Why Goal Setting Works

One way that goal setting drives better performance is in how goals provide for greater focus. Locke and Latham's (2017) extensive research on goal setting suggests that

- articulating our aims also helps to ensure more significant levels of motivation and drive,
- having established goals produces more tenacity to reach the desired outcomes,

- having tighter time frames for completion helps to increase production even more than a longer deadline might, and
- having goals contributes to using existing knowledge and seeking further learning.

Part Three of this book explores even more the pursuit of further learning through PKM. Aligning our goals with our ability to leverage existing knowledge and further develop our learning is a vital aspect of being productive.

Three Types of Goal Setting

Following are the three, broad types of goal setting:

1. Time based: Takes place at specified intervals
2. Project based: Occurs around a specific project or aim
3. Feedback based: Evolves based on feedback received from course evaluations; performance reviews (including tenure or promotion processes); or other ways we solicit input from students, colleagues, or other stakeholders

Time-Based Goal Setting
Goals may be established or reviewed at various intervals.

Annually
The most well-known type of goal setting is performed annually. As indicated previously, yearly goals can present challenges. The circumstances under which the goals were set can shift drastically between intervals. The goals can

become meaningless because the context in which they were established is no longer relevant.

However, there are some excellent uses for annual goal setting. Mapping out one's tenure or promotion process can be helpful. Another focus can be on publications or other types of scholarship. Blocking out the significant goals that need to be attained to achieve a broader goal can be useful in articulating what needs to occur in a given year. Even more beneficial would be to break those more substantial achievements into smaller pieces.

Trimesterly

An emerging way to approach setting goals is to shorten the duration of time to less than a year. In *The 12 Week Year: Get More Done in 12 Weeks Than Others Do in 12 Months*, Moran and Lennington (2013) take issue with annualized planning. They suggest that planning take place in 12-week increments, which "creates focus and clarity on what matters most and a sense of urgency to do it now" (p. 67). Instead of the surge of motivation that we can feel in December as we consider all that is possible in the coming year, we get to experience that renewed focus and sense of urgency every 12 weeks.

Some academics have modified the idea of the 12-week year to accommodate the structure of an academic year. Those who teach in semesters can have two 15-week years (to use the vernacular) and a summer-long year.

Monthly

Kruse (2017) recommends establishing a monthly theme to help keep our focus on what is essential. He describes how having a theme helps him determine which tasks deserve his attention.

> It just narrows the to-do-list down to a smaller and smaller funnel so you can make better decisions and be quicker about it, as opposed to getting lost in your to-do list or being overwhelmed by seeing every little thing scheduled in your calendar and a slight deviation throws the whole game off. (para. 5)

Project-Based Goal Setting

Goals can also be related to specific projects. When designing a new course, we might have goals regarding implementing universal design for learning principles into a new course or incorporating video in a new way we have not tried in the past. When writing goals for projects, articulate the desired end state.

Feedback-Based Goal Setting

After reviewing course evaluations or after someone has evaluated one of our online courses is an ideal time to identify any goals that are needed to make improvements to the class. Sometimes the feedback warrants only small changes that can be captured by recording a few next actions. However, deeper issues may be uncovered when we receive feedback on our work, and having a clearly identified goal can help us be more specific about where we want to head.

GTD: AN OVERVIEW

As articulated in the introduction, productive online professors are aware of those actions they have committed to and what is most important for them to accomplish. We have enough room in our lives for the unexpected things to arise. We also have systems that make our work flow better to best capitalize on the time we invest in serving our students well and pursuing our goals. Broadly speaking, we want to take action on those priorities that are most important in our lives.

The one book that has influenced my productivity approaches more than any other is Allen's (2015) *Getting Things Done*. The following overview introduces the vocabulary and practices of GTD. Allen's book is among those that are included within the recommended reading section on the Thrive Online website (thriveonlineseries .com). *The Productive Online and Offline Professor* provides specific guidance on incorporating GTD into a higher education context.

An important tenet of GTD is articulated in this quote from Allen (2015): "The mind is for having ideas, not holding them" (p. 277). It is easy to discern the inadequacies of the human mind for remembering things as we think through a typical day of an online professor. Let's call her Juanita. Juanita might

- receive more than 90 emails in her inbox,
- conduct two online sessions for her classes,
- interact with her family,

- attend a committee meeting to evaluate a new educational technology tool,
- write two recommendation letters for past students,
- develop a proposal to speak at a conference,
- go to the dentist,
- work on designing a new course, and
- explore buying a new hard drive.

Each one of these items might have multiple follow-up items associated with them. Perhaps she volunteered to try the educational technology tool in one of her online courses next term. She will need to capture that commitment somewhere, so she will not forget about it. Maybe she wants to ask her information technology (IT) department if there is a less expensive option for her hard drive. If she knows that she will be on campus visiting the library tomorrow, which is right next to the IT department, she can set her task manager app to remind her when she is in the vicinity. One of the students who requested a letter of recommendation may have left out information that she needs to complete the request. She can request the data from the student as well as consider creating a form for students to fill out when requesting references to reduce the likelihood of this delay happening again in the future. Using some of the approaches articulated in GTD will help Juanita avoid relying solely on her memory to do the necessary follow-up. Instead, she can allow trusted GTD systems to be the brains of her operation, freeing her own mind for more creative work.

In the upcoming sections, discover how to capture thoughts and actions, clarify their meaning and significance, create an organizational system, take time to reflect and review goals and priorities, and then actually execute on plans and actions.

Invitation to Connect

What do you anticipate the most challenging part of establishing a GTD system might be for you? Share your thoughts using #ThriveOnline.

Capture

Because our minds are not really equipped to store ideas indefinitely, we set up systems that can capture ideas and actions as we have them or as they are presented to us by others. Instead of attempting to recall each outstanding task in our minds, we record those actions in our trusted system. It is useful to regularly transfer those tasks that are cluttering our minds into our task manager, calendar, goals list, and other elements of GTD.

We mistrust our brains to remember all the potential actions that will come our way daily. However, because we know that we will have an opportunity to evaluate each item that we capture at designated times, we trust that those issues will be reliably addressed.

The goal is to use the brain for more important functions than trying to remember things. The discipline of capturing frees up the mind for embarking on more creative pursuits. The following are the primary ways to think about the act of capturing: (a) sometimes we respond to stuff that is coming at us (whether we want it to or not) and (b) it can be helpful to more proactively reflect on what has been going on and what actions need to be moved into our GTD system.

The Stuff Coming at Us

As online professors, there is stuff coming at us all day. We receive emails from students and colleagues, our learning management systems (LMSs) ping us with assignments that need to be graded, we discover a new journal article that will be good to incorporate into our class, or we receive a calendar invite to an upcoming committee meeting. It can be overwhelming to know what to do with all of the various potential inputs into how we might spend our time.

One of the ways that stuff flies at us is via our inboxes. Instead of a single inbox at work for incoming paperwork, we now have multiple ways information and requests can enter our lives. There are email inboxes, voicemails, hallway conversations that result in us making impromptu commitments, and social media communication.

Our students reach out to us at all hours of the day, every day of the week. Scheduled online videoconferences introduce even more potential for needed follow-up. In Box 1.1 Luis's process of capture demonstrates how we might identify those items that require our attention.

Inboxes help to facilitate the capture process. I remember when I had a single inbox. It sat on my desk at work back in the early 1990s. Today, I have multiple email inboxes, physical inboxes that sit on my desk at work and on my home office credenza, social media inboxes

Instead of attempting to recall each outstanding task in our minds, we record those actions in our trusted system.

#ThriveOnline

Box 1.1 Case Example: Part One

Luis finishes his scheduled videoconference with his Introduction to Biology course and saves the chat messages as a file in his virtual inbox to look at the next time he performs his weekly review. Then, he will be able to identify any items that require follow-up from their session.

Luis compares a few different webcam options and adds the information in his notes app about the various models and which one he prefers. He is aware that he will need to purchase the webcam soon so that it will arrive before he holds his next synchronous session.

Luis just started reading a new introduction to biology text that he is considering adopting for future courses. He received an evaluation copy from the publisher and added it to his electronic reading materials on his tablet. Luis forwards the email from the publisher with the link to the e-textbook to his task manager so he can track his progress in evaluating the book within the broader context of his work.

When he is on a videoconference with one of his students, he jots down a quick note that he should consider providing an explainer video on anabolic and catabolic processes to the entire class because this student is not likely the only person with a question. He places the note in his physical inbox, which will be revisited the next time he goes through it.

Note that in these various capture processes, Luis has placed items in several inboxes. Most of Luis's inboxes are digital, although he also has physical inboxes.

(*Continues*)

Box 1.1 (*Continued*)

> He has a folder on his computer called /1-inbox (how to name files and folders is addressed in Part Five of *The Productive Online and Offline Professor*), which he uses to place files that require additional follow-up. He uses the drafts app on his phone to capture quick notes that he does not want to miss instead of worrying about where to put the information or what to do with it. Any note-type app could serve the same purpose for him, but Luis appreciates the simplicity of opening the app and having a blank draft note, ready for an idea or action to be captured.
>
> Although much of Luis's work takes place virtually, he does still have physical inboxes (one at home and one at his university office). Most of the time, he captures the commitments that are represented by the items that are in his physical inboxes (e.g., the note that he wrote about sending the video to his class) and then recycles the paper. Occasionally, he needs to scan the documents and keep them for later reference.

(Twitter, Facebook, LinkedIn, etc.), and a couple of inboxes associated with various apps. Allen (2015) recommends in articulating the GTD system that we have as many inboxes as we need, and no more than that. One of the practices that really helped me was to realize that my physical inboxes at work and at home were underutilized, but since I travel back and forth between offices and classrooms much of the week, I could make use of other kinds of inboxes for paperwork, too. I carry a plastic folder around in my computer bag that is an inbox for anything a student may hand me during an in-person class, or an important handout distributed during a meeting. I consider my phone's voicemail an inbox as well. See Figure 1.1 for examples of inboxes.

We have relatively little control over the flurry of items coming into these various inboxes. The descriptions of the capture process thus far have regarded more reactionary methods. A student's need was identified, so an action item was captured. An online session concluded, and a file with potential follow-up was saved in a virtual inbox folder. These items were captured because of an interaction or an in-the-moment thought.

GTD also prescribes a more purposeful emptying of one's mind through what Allen (2015) calls "the mind sweep" (p. 114). After the various inboxes have been cleared, our minds are likely still full of actions that have had our attention but were not included in what we already captured. Allen recommends getting out a stack of paper and writing what comes to mind on separate sheets. Each piece of paper represents an item being emptied out of our minds, as we think of it. Other more digitally minded GTD practitioners recommend the

Figure 1.1. Various types of inboxes.

INBOXES

virtual equivalent of paper, such as a simple note app or mind-mapping application. See the Thrive Online website at thriveonlineseries.com for examples of recommended note-taking and mind-mapping applications.

The resulting set of items will likely fall into completely random categories. The personal will mix with the professional. The larger-in-scope, two-year projects will blend in with the need to purchase new gardening gloves for this weekend.

Instead of relying on some idea to emerge organically, or waiting for someone else to call something to our attention that requires action, we can prime the pump through the use of an incompletion triggers list. Reading through the items on the list can trigger us to consider what needs to be attended to without us having to come up with it in the first place. A professional triggers list for an online instructor could include the following:

- Class planning
- Upcoming synchronous/scheduled class meetings
- Grading
- Professional development
- Research
- Conferences
- Forthcoming meetings

Reading through those triggers might help us anticipate the online learning task force's meeting that is coming up in a couple of weeks. It also could get us thinking about the conference we hope to attend early next year.

Allen's (2015) personal list includes a section related to health:

Health

- Doctors
- Dentist
- Optometrist
- Healthcare specialists
- Checkups
- Diet
- Food
- Exercise (p. 119)

Reviewing this list can help identify an aspect of our health that is being neglected. It might be a trigger to try a new exercise class at the gym or schedule a trip to the farmers' market this weekend. The fact that scheduling of the dentist appointment is still overdue will also be brought to our attention.

Capturing is an essential part of any trusted system. Various inboxes (virtual and physical ones) can capture things that need to be taken care of. As we interact with people throughout the day (online, over email, and in person), actions will be identified that require our attention. A triggers list can also be used to generate even more steps that need to be taken to follow through on our commitments and keep parts of our lives from getting out of control.

Clarify

The process of capturing can generate even more stress (look at all the stuff that needs doing!) unless time is invested clarifying what actions need to be taken or what the collected items mean. Clarifying transforms the various items that have been captured into actions with specific steps and aims. We must ask ourselves, "What precisely is this 'thing' we have captured and is it actionable?"

Actionable items get done right away (if we can take care of it quickly), delegated to others, deferred until a later time, or put into our task manager to do as soon as feasible. Crafting these next actions as precisely as possible is paramount.

Use a verb to articulate the step that needs to be taken with each of the items that have been captured. Here are some examples of action items related to an online instructor who is in the process of converting these artifacts from the various inboxes into next actions:

- Grade: My ethical framework assignments from BUSN435
- Schedule: Time to meet with department chair about next semester's classes
- Apply: To present at the Instructure (makers of the Canvas LMS) conference
- Edit: Closed captions for My Ethical Framework video introduction

Each of these tasks has a definite point at which you could determine what "done" looks like. Either I graded those assignments or I did not. Either the meeting has been scheduled or I am waiting on a response. This goes back to having a system we can trust in which we are able to know exactly what needs to be done in order for us to move closer to accomplishing our goals.

Dini (2014) even takes it as far as recommending that we not create a dishonest task management system. That is, do not say we are going to *do* a task if what we truly mean is that we are going to *consider doing* a task. For example, we could use a more definitive verb, as in "Finish: Taking online course." However, because we are aware that we are not going to finish that in one sitting, we should craft the task more realistically, such as "Consider: Watching portion of online course," and then set this task up to be deferred another two or three days. I use this approach when deciding whether or not to attend an upcoming conference. Instead of stating in my task manager, "Apply to present at the Lilly Conference," I enter, "Consider applying to present at the Lilly Conference." If I look at that task in the context of all the other actions I have captured, I may very well decide that (given my other priorities) I do not have the time to create a proposal this year. I can mark that task as complete, knowing that I did consider it—I just did not actually do it. Box 1.2 continues Luis's example, showing the progress he is making in managing his to-do list.

The clarifying process involves actionable items as well as those that do not have a specific required step. Those nonactionable items might be something we can just trash, might belong in a reference system, or might be better placed in what in GTD parlance is known as a someday/maybe list.

How to structure digital files is addressed in Part Five, for those who want more inspiration on how to organize this aspect of online instruction. Trash (or recycle) unneeded documentation. If getting rid of instructions for something that may be needed down the road proves

Box 1.2 Case Example: Part Two

Following is a list of items that Luis captured in the earlier section of this case, along with how he could further detail each of those items during the clarify process:

1. Chat text file from online class session from /1-inbox folder: Identify actions that Luis needs to follow up on. (Email students virtual lab description and clarifications on the first exam. Ask Linda to share a link to her video. Verify that Adam is indeed registered in the course at this point.)

2. Drafts app entry (note) about his webcam comparisons: Decide on and purchase webcam action item entered in task manager.

3. Email from the publisher (now located in task manager) about potential new textbook: Evaluate Introduction to Biology textbook.

4. Note about possibly creating an explainer video about anabolic and catabolic processes: Consider: Creating an explainer video about anabolic and catabolic processes. (Notice that Luis does not state that he is, in fact, going to create the video. Sometimes we can get a little ahead of ourselves. We have just finished conducting an in-person or virtual class and might anticipate that we have more time to devote to our inspirations than we have. If Luis committed to the student that he would create the video, of course he should go ahead and fulfill his obligation.

(Continues)

Box 1.2 (*Continued*)

> However, if it was more of a brainstorm he thought to himself, he will be able to revisit this idea in the context of the larger tasks and projects the next time he looks at them during a weekly or monthly review.)
>
> None of Luis's action items took less than a couple of minutes to do. Otherwise, he would have just done the tasks right then and there. Instead, they were all recorded in his task manager for evaluation among the other commitments he has captured. He was not able to delegate any of them. Yes, they may be essential and should be done soon. However, none of them had specific dates by which they required completion, as would be the case for a conference presentation proposal or a course being launched on the first day of a new term.

too mentally challenging, at least get the documentation into digital form where it will avoid cluttering up physical surroundings. Do a Google search for the documentation to see if it is already available in an electronic form, so you can rest easy recycling the paper copy. If it is not available, use an app on a smartphone to scan it. For larger jobs a desktop scanner may be used. Recommendations for scanning apps and hardware are included on thriveonlineseries.com.

Place items inside a someday/maybe list to keep your task manager free from being a brainstorming tool, and instead one that is used to attend to actual commitments and projects. See Figure 1.2 for a sample someday/maybe list.

Figure 1.2. Sample someday/maybe list.

Someday/Maybe list

PROFESSIONAL DEVELOPMENT

- Take Coursera Learning How to Learn Course
- Continue Mastering Zoom Course
- Read *Minds Online* by Michelle Miller

TECHNOLOGY

- Consider switching to feedbin for RSS feeds
- Explore Zapier + Alfred
- Evaluate BetterTouchTool application

TEACHING

- Evaluate taking sides book(s) for BUSN435
- Create a course trailer for BUSN435
- Explore Cornell University's Center for Teaching Excellence's teaching and learning book list

PERSONAL

- Try foam roller stretches for plantar fasciitis
- Consider buying outdoor console storage unit
- Check out info on apple picking in Oak Glen

A someday/maybe list can be categorized into different sections. Consider including a section for ideas on how to improve your teaching, another for ideas that are related to specific courses, or even one that lists places you want to explore with your family during an upcoming holiday break.

Organize

Anyone obsessed with the television series *Clean Sweep* (van Riet, 2003) from the early 2000s will have had it drummed into their head that each item in our homes needs a place. It is so much easier to keep things organized when we know where to place stuff we plan on keeping and where to retrieve stuff when we need to use it, or reference it, again. This method of organization can be employed both with physical items and with digital stuff.

Allen (2015) recommends having the following systems of organization:

- Someday/maybe list (discussed in the prior section)
- Reference (explored in Parts Three and Five)
- Waiting (a way of tracking those items that have been delegated to others)
- Calendar (discussed later in Part One and also in Part Five)
- Next actions (otherwise known as a task manager task management system)
- Projects (list of all the projects, which are established each time an outcome will require more than one action to complete)
- Project plans (the action items that fall underneath each project and are tracked typically in a task manager)

Having those lists on hand has been a major contributor to my own sense of knowing what is important and not having essential commitments go unmet. However, seeing how they are put to use is crucial. Box 1.3 will catch us up with Luis in the third part of this example.

As we capture and clarify, we can place actions and reference items in places that will make it easy for us to pay attention to these items when they become most relevant to us. Our organization systems should be continually evolving as our needs change and as our various roles require us to take on new responsibilities.

As information, requests, and ideas flow into our lives, we need a way of refining those into what requires action on our part or what else we may want to do with those things. Figure 1.3 shows a GTD workflow example of the process of capturing, clarifying, and organizing items:

- Items are captured through calls, emails, ideas, meetings, and so on.
- Items are clarified by determining their significance and whether they are actionable.
- Items are organized by placing them in the appropriate place—a virtual folder, added as a new project, placed on a calendar, and so on.

Reflect

Thus far in the process, we have captured our ideas, tasks, voicemails, and next actions. We then have clarified how each of these items has meaning to us and what needs to be completed. Finally, we have refined our organization

Box 1.3 Case Example: Part Three

When we last left Luis, he had captured several task pieces through various inboxes and interactions. He articulated those items as next actions and placed them within his task manager. He already has an organization system set up, but he may find as he works with it that it requires tweaking, or things need to be moved around. If Luis decides that he does not have time to complete as extensive of an explainer video as he would like to this term, he can move that item from his task manager over to his someday/maybe list.

When Luis first requested the textbook from the publisher, he could have added an item to his Waiting list, such as "Waiting for: Introduction to Biology textbook desk copy from publisher." All other items that he has delegated to others are on this same list, making it easy to reference what commitments are still outstanding.

Luis uses Evernote to store the research he has been doing on which webcam to purchase. As he is looking at various models, he uses the Evernote screen clipper to grab screenshots, pricing information, and detailed specs from the multiple vendors' websites. Distraction ensues during his online shopping. Luis becomes tempted by a new professional-grade microphone. Instead of getting bogged down with a task that does not require his immediate attention (and is outside the range of his gadget budget), Luis adds it to his someday/maybe list and remains focused on the most imperative purchase for his more immediate needs.

Figure 1.3. GTD workflow example.

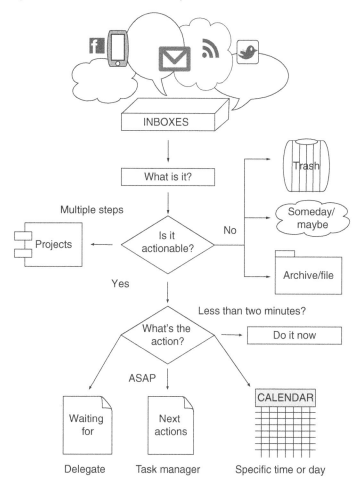

system, such that each item has a "bucket" to land in and we have rid ourselves of the feeling that we have to tackle each item as it catches our attention.

Instead of diving into doing all the tasks that have arrived in our to-do list, we need time for reflection. It is this crucial process that causes us to reconsider our priorities, assess how our systems are working for us, and determine whether we are making progress on our projects.

Conduct Reviews

Conducting regular reviews gives us the opportunity to reflect and avoid spending too much time in a reactionary mode. Talbert (2017a) stresses the importance of having a plan:

> Planning matters, because we need some structure in life in order to get the most out of our lives. . . . We want to know that our work is meaningful and that the meaning of our work is somehow congruent to the meaning of our lives. (para. 5)

One of the ways we can reflect is by conducting periodic reviews. These are the times during which we review our projects to ensure that they are not stalled, we reflect on how we are doing at achieving our goals, and we even allow ourselves to dream a bit about what the future may hold. As I consider the value that reviews have brought to me, I am reminded of a vivid example, depicted in Box 1.4.

Instead of diving right into doing all the tasks that have arrived in our to-do list, we need time for reflection.

#ThriveOnline

Box 1.4 The Relief a Weekly Review Brings

We were dealing with a stressful family matter. I had a relative who had been diagnosed with dementia. We had just determined that a neighbor had stolen substantial portions of my family member's income in recent years. We were all trying to thwart the woman's attempts to take even more of my relative's money. There were many emotional turns during a particularly difficult weekend, and by the time I arrived at our university to teach classes on that Monday, I was exhausted.

My mind was filled with a flurry of all the tasks I was behind on from the prior week. I had just secured my first-ever book contract and had gotten behind on my writing schedule. My role had changed at my institution, but I was still teaching courses to finish out the semester under the old arrangement. I was also teaching for my occasional adjunct position in a doctoral program at a different institution. Those online students had a plethora of questions as they embarked on their primary research paper for the course.

I had not slept very well the night before, and my eyes hurt. The caffeine from my morning's iced tea had not kicked in yet. As I hooked up my computer to my external monitor, I made the unwise decision to open my email application. In fluttered more than 40 emails, and it was only 9:15 a.m. I was stressed.

My self-discipline suddenly kicked in. I closed the email back down and opened up my task management

---

(*Continues*)

Box 1.4 (*Continued*)

system. I accessed my weekly review workflow and started to step through each of the actions I take each week to prioritize my tasks and get current with my obligations. The process helped me take stock of what was going to be most pressing for me to tackle before I went off and taught my first class of the day. My breathing started to become slower. I felt the transformation in my body from symptoms of stress to a sense of renewed energy. I was ready to begin my week and better prepared to address any of the inevitable unplanned actions that would come up as a result of the situation with my family member that week.

The Weekly Review

Allen (2015) prescribes a process of review at regular intervals. He describes how performing a weekly review better enables us to align our daily actions with the bigger picture:

> Very simply, the weekly review is whatever you need to do to get your head empty again and get oriented for the next couple of weeks. It's going through the steps of workflow management—capturing, clarifying, organizing and reviewing all your outstanding commitments, intentions, and inclinations—until you can honestly say, "I absolutely know right now everything I'm not doing but could be doing if I decided to." (p. 195)

Allen (2015) recommends a three-step process for performing a weekly review: Get clear, get current, and get creative. In this section, I describe my weekly review process to give you a sense of how these can be structured. However, the weekly review is a set of tasks that will look different for each person. The process of weekly review may seem overwhelming to you at first, but you can easily decide that your weekly review will need to start out more simplified than what you see outlined here. Once you have established a routine and have started to experience the benefits of reflective work, you may find that you want to increase the number of items that you look at during your weekly review to receive even more positive results from the process. Figure 1.4 reflects the kinds of actions taken during a person's weekly review.

My weekly review changes over time as well. When I find an action that seems to get lost in the shuffle and is causing issues, I consider adding it to my review steps. I reflect on how well my weekly review process is working every few months and make any necessary adjustments. The time invested to stop and reflect on this particular workflow has produced worthwhile results each time I have stepped back and reviewed my reviews.

I found that my computer desktop was regularly getting cluttered. I sometimes place files there when working on a project but then forget to move them to the folder to which they belong. My weekly review changed to incorporate the action of clearing the files that were left on my desktop. Now I know that at least once a week my desktop will be cleared and my files will be properly organized within my folder structure.

Figure 1.4. Sample weekly review.

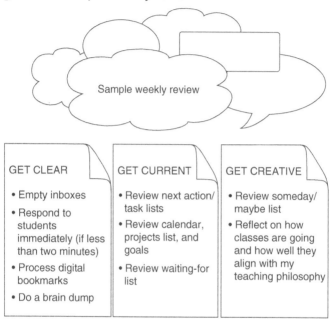

Sample weekly review

GET CLEAR

- Empty inboxes
- Respond to students immediately (if less than two minutes)
- Process digital bookmarks
- Do a brain dump

GET CURRENT

- Review next action/ task lists
- Review calendar, projects list, and goals
- Review waiting-for list

GET CREATIVE

- Review someday/ maybe list
- Reflect on how classes are going and how well they align with my teaching philosophy

Get Clear

I used to be a complete stacker. If you came into my home office, there would be stacks and stacks of papers all over the (ideally) open space of my desk. I had an L-shaped desk, plus a large filing cabinet. A ton of stacks could fit in that space before there was any danger of not having enough room for them. The inevitable problem came when something was in one of those stacks that required action. Things eventually got so bad with my stacking that there was overflow in a linen closet that was just outside my home office.

When my husband and I got married, we went off on our honeymoon without me realizing there was an unpaid credit card inside the linen closet stack. There was a ding on my credit card and a bruise to my ego. I had prided myself on having an excellent credit score and on being responsible for financial matters.

The happy ending to this story is that my habits have changed. I knew that my system (or lack of a system) was no longer workable.

One of the many new habits I needed was a set of actions to help me clear out any "small stacks" that were starting to form in the various "inboxes" I had. I placed those words in quotes because sometimes these "stacks" came in the form of virtual inboxes, such as email inboxes. By taking these steps weekly, I avoided any urgent tasks (like paying credit card bills) from not catching my attention in time to attend to them.

Use the following sample getting clear process to design one that works for you:

Process inboxes. These inboxes might be physical or virtual inboxes that should be cleared out every week to prevent failing to record any necessary actions in a task manager. Here is a list of inboxes that I clear out weekly to get you started. Feel free to modify them to fit your situation:

- *Task manager*: Many electronic to-do lists have a feature that allows emails to be forwarded or entered into the task manager's inbox. The body of the email becomes a note in the task manager and the subject line becomes the name of the to-do. Edits can be made later within the task manager. Process this inbox by providing information along with the task, such as what project it is associated with, when it is due, and if there are any specifics as to where you need to be or what tools you need to use to complete the task (context).

- *Emails*: Empty each email address's inbox. Delete the email, archive it for future reference, reply to the email if it takes less than two minutes, or forward the email to your task manager's inbox.
- *Evernote*: This notebook application also has an inbox for those notes you captured in the moment and did not appropriately categorize. Once a week, go in and clear out the inbox, putting every note into the proper notebook and applying the relevant tags (e.g., the course the item relates to or the topic).
- *Home office*: Any physical mail you receive during the week or other items that are gathered at home can go into your home office inbox. Clear it out by tossing out items; filing them, mostly by scanning them and getting them in a digital repository; or getting them into your task management system if they have a due date associated with them or some action is required.
- *University*: You may also have a physical inbox at the institution where you teach that you can go through as described for your home office.

- *Portable*: Keep a folder in your computer bag that is labeled "Inbox" to use for papers you collect throughout your day. All items collected in this folder should be cleared out each week.
- *Drafts app*: This app is designed for capturing notes without worrying about where they go. Once a week, I process any notes stored in my drafts app and move them to where they belong. These notes might be sent to Evernote for archiving purposes, to my task manager to turn into an action, or even added to my list of movies to watch on the Internet Movie Database (IMDb; imdb.com).
- *Digital files*: Process any inboxes you have set up for digital files. As I download files during a given week, they often wind up in my default downloads folder or sometimes they are even left on my computer's desktop. Throughout the week, I often move these files over to a folder I created called 1-inbox. I use the number "1" so it will be placed at the top of the list of files when viewing items alphabetically. Once a week, I go through the 1-inbox and move files over to their more permanent digital home on my computer. (In Part Five, you will discover how to manage files and folders more effectively, to streamline this process.)

Process bookmarks. Getting clear also involves taking a look at the bookmarks that I have saved during the week and adding any needed tags. Most often, I add tags when I am saving a bookmark. However, I have my digital bookmark tool (Pinboard.in) set up to automatically add any items that I flag as my favorites on Twitter to my list of bookmarks. It is incredibly fast to add a resource for future reference, but this does require that I go back once a week during my weekly review and make this information more easily accessible by adding relevant tags.

Do a brain dump. The final step is perhaps the most vital for me. The brain dump is when I empty my head of any actions that I have yet to capture in my task manager, add in new projects that have emerged in the prior week, enter any items in my waiting-for lists that I have delegated to others, and record any items on my someday/maybe list.

Get Current

The next part of my weekly review involves getting current. This is the phase where lists and reminders are updated or deleted. Those using an analog system get the amazing feeling of checking that item off on a task list.

Any stress I have been experiencing from feeling overwhelmed usually starts to come way down after I have gone through my process of getting clear. Hard-copy documents have been scanned (using my scanner or scanning app on my smartphone) and either shredded, recycled, or occasionally filed (which I typically do only if there is a requirement for the document to be kept in hard copy form). This clears the clutter of not only my physical environment but also my digital realm. There is a trusted system at work, helping me remain aware of the actions that need to be taken in the near term and keeping future actions out of sight until they become relevant again.

Review next action lists. During a given week, there are times when I am moving so fast that I neglect to mark off specific actions that I have completed. I ensure that my next action list is accurate during this phase. Much of the time, I take this step at the same time as I am performing a brain dump. As I add action items into my various projects, I also often notice that some of the steps have been completed or are no longer critical in achieving my desired outcomes.

Review goals. Regularly reviewing progress toward goals is vital to my ability to achieve what I have set out to do. It is also a significant way to prioritize what is most important to focus on in the coming week.

Review projects list. I consider each class I teach as a project. When I revise a course (which happens almost every time I teach), that becomes a project. Anything that requires multiple actions to get to a desired outcome is a project. Reviewing my list of projects is vital in determining what may be holding me back from achieving a goal, or how to prioritize my time in a given week.

Review calendar. Allen (2015) writes, "Your calendar is one of the best checklists to review regularly, to prevent last-minute stress and trigger creative front-end thinking" (p. 196). Per Allen's advice, I look at calendar data from the prior and upcoming weeks. Looking back a week, I can see if there are any items I have committed to that have yet to be recorded in my system. My preference is to capture any action items during the actual meetings I attend, but inevitably I will miss some and am grateful for the opportunity to double-check that nothing is missing in my task manager. Looking out a week allows me to see what meetings and events are coming up and to plan accordingly.

Review waiting-for list. My waiting-for list helps me track any action items that I have delegated to others or that require others to accomplish. My task manager lists general waiting-for items, such as "Waiting: Payment for webinar" or "Waiting: Reply on podcast guest profile form request." It also contains waiting-for lists that are directed at specific people, such as my husband, my teaching assistant, the person to whom I report, or my direct reports.

Get Creative

Allen (2015) stresses that we do not endure the weekly review solely to get things cleaned up. It is also essential to access untapped creativity and deep thinking that otherwise is not possible when living in chaos. He writes, "We are naturally creative beings, invested in our existence to list, grow, express, and expand. The challenge is not to be creative—it is to eliminate the barriers to the natural flow of our creative energies" (p. 198).

The processes of getting clear and current already allow us to be creative in ways we might not have realized. Instead of reacting to whatever comes our way via email and responding to others' demands and requests, we reflect on what is important and how to align our work with our most profound sense of purpose.

Review someday/maybe list. I enjoy the process of adding items to my someday/maybe list as well as taking a look at it once a week to see if anything is worth exploring in the coming week. There is inadequate time to experiment with every technology tool that I discover, but I know that my someday/maybe list will remind me to experiment with other tools when I am in a better position to do so, given all my other priorities.

My someday/maybe list (see Figure 1.2) has the following various categories of possibilities:

- Professional development
- Technology
- Teaching
- Personal

When I review my someday/maybe list, I am in the frame of mind to explore creative possibilities. Having a place to store these percolating ideas is helpful to avoid getting distracted by them when I am not in a space to do anything with the inspiration.

Monthly Reviews

My monthly reviews look very similar to my weekly reviews. However, it is at this time that I do a more thorough review of our finances. I check to see how much we budgeted to spend in the prior month and how much was actually spent. As I look forward to the coming month, I consider what expenses are coming and what behavioral changes may need to occur or what money decisions may need to be made to help us meet our financial goals. Some people may need to include financial check-ups in their weekly reviews, but we have been budgeting for long enough that monthly reviews are adequate for our family.

Trimesterly Reviews

Going from monthly reviews to annual reviews can often be too big of a jump for the kinds of opportunities for reflection these reviews provide. Instead of 12 monthly reviews and an annual review, we can consider the larger picture by having 3 more substantial reviews per year. Many of us have 2 semesters and 1 summer break and can plan around those seasons for bigger picture reviews. Talbert (2017b) refers to these types of check-ins as trimesterly reviews and recommends that we give ourselves 3 opportunities each year to conduct a broader review of our progress toward goals. There are many ways we might carve out time for reviewing, but the important thing is that we regularly find opportunities for this kind of reflection and planning.

Engage

The prior steps we have taken enable us to engage most fully with our most important work. We have captured, clarified, organized, and reflected. Now it is time to get to work actually doing. All the tasks that were uncovered while reading email that took more than two minutes to complete show up in our task list. Those actions that came to mind when going through the triggers list are listed.

One of the challenges to this phase can be determining where to start. All too often, we wind up feeling even more overwhelmed and unclear on where to focus our attention. The weekly review can be a time during which we identify what will come first when we get to a more unstructured time of our week.

A helpful practice can be to identify three to five next actions that, at a minimum, will be completed during a given day. Some task managers include an indication of what kind of focus might be required to complete a task. We need deep focus for writing but can fold laundry even when our mind is exhausted. Attend to those items that need ample focus during the time of the day when you have the most energy. Save those tasks that can be achieved with less energy for the lull so many of us have in the late afternoon.

During times when more focus is required, I block out time on my calendar to make progress on specific projects and action items. My task manager (OmniFocus) allows me to drag an individual task onto my calendar application, saving me the time of having to type in how I plan on spending that time. By default, the application devotes an hour to the task, but I can adjust the duration to better match the time required.

Invitation to Connect

Share an approach that has worked well for working on tasks that align with your focus and energy level on a given day using #ThriveOnline.

SELECTING AND SETTING UP A TASK MANAGER

In the Goal Setting section, we explored three types of goals: time based, project based, and feedback based. If you are early in experimenting with goal setting as a

All too often, we wind up feeling even more overwhelmed and unclear on where to focus our attention.

#ThriveOnline

means for increasing your productivity, I find that people in higher education can usually wrap their minds around the items they need to complete that are associated with the "seasons" of an academic year (whether your institution uses a semester, quarterly, or some other schedule). Consider reflecting on what goals you have established or take some time to record them now. Having a list of your aims will help as you consider selecting and setting up a task manager.

Once goals have been established, it is time to determine the steps needed to reach those aims. The tools used to track the needed actions are often called *task managers* or *task management systems*. This section outlines two broad types of task managers: analog systems (that are handwritten) and digital systems (that involve technology). In selecting a tool, it is good to check out what is out there, but ultimately select one that meets your unique needs.

Whether we are using an analog or a digital tool, it is best to use one that is designed for task management. Just because a tool can track actions does not mean it will make a good task manager. I taught computer applications courses early in my career and have seen all sorts of misuses of technology that arose from not understanding the primary purpose for a given tool. Yes, Excel can act in some ways like Microsoft Word, but it truly does not perform the job of word processing anywhere near as well as a tool that was built for that. You can try to use Excel as a database. However, if you want a form where someone else inputs information and it becomes a part of your data

Just because a tool can track actions does not mean it will make a good task manager.

#ThriveOnline

set, you are going to want to look into a database application because that is what they are designed to do.

A calendar does not make for a great way of tracking tasks that need to be done. Many of our actions as online professors are not time based. We need to finish grading, but it does not have to happen at 11:00 a.m. on Thursdays. As discussed in Part Two, email is also a poor way to track action items. What we need is a tool that is explicitly designed to manage projects and tasks. The tool we select should also suit our individual needs and preferences. Having to remember to return a student's call or to apply for a fellowship ties up our brain's horsepower. What we want is a task manager to do that heavy lifting, freeing up our minds for more creative pursuits (e.g., brainstorming ideas for a new class we will be teaching).

Analog Task Management Systems

Paper-based task managers work well for those who prefer a more tactile, analog experience in keeping track of actions and projects. One of the most significant factors in determining whether a digital or an analog task management system is appropriate is whether or not a person will commit to carrying it around everywhere. Otherwise, the capturing, clarifying, and organizing processes that have been described will likely suffer.

There are two basic types of analog options for task managers: task managers that are built from scratch by following a prescribed methodology and planners that are printed and designed around a specific system for task management and other types of planning.

Build-Your-Own Task Managers

A task manager can be built out of paper and a binder clip and does not need to cost a fortune. The Hipster PDA system started this way, with a recipe for how to fold and fill in blank sheets of paper as a means for organizing one's self. Mann (2004), of inbox zero fame, first conceived this organizer and it went through multiple iterations as it grew in popularity. Mann describes the beauty and simplicity of the Hipster PDA as follows:

> The Hipster PDA (Parietal Disgorgement Aid) is a fully extensible system for coordinating incoming and outgoing data for any aspect of your life and work. It scales brilliantly, degrades gracefully, supports optional categories and "beaming," and is configurable to an unlimited number of options. Best of all, the Hipster PDA fits into your hip pocket and costs practically nothing to purchase and maintain. Let's make one together. (para. 2)

He goes on to describe that we need to get a stack of three-inch-by-five-inch cards, then use a clip to bind them together. "There is no step three" (Mann, 2004, para. 3). Those wishing for more guidance than that are in luck. The Internet is full of options for how to populate a Hipster PDA, including a do-it-yourself planner Hipster PDA, with forms that can be printed onto index cards and used for implementing a GTD system.

Another build-it-yourself task manager is the bullet journal. Ryder Carroll (n.d.) created this approach to note-taking and task management. One of the keys to the bullet journal is in how symbols are used to indicate the type of information being conveyed through the note-taking process. The key section is like the legend of your journal, and you will use it to decipher what is ahead. Here's how a writer for the *Los Angeles Times* described his legend system:

• A black dot indicates a task.

> A forward arrow means a task that has migrated over from a previous list or month.

< A less-than sign indicates a task that has been scheduled for a specific time.

○ A circle means an event.

— A dash is a note to one's self.

* A star adds special importance to a note.

Drawing an eye means "look into" (Florez, 2016, para. 11)

The bullet journal legend may be used in planners you construct yourself or within a planner system that is designed to capture task lists, calendars, journaling, and other functions.

Custom-Printed Planners

Those who desire a less do-it-yourself approach might enjoy one of the custom analog planners that are available to purchase. This section shares some of the more popular planners. More information is also available on the Thrive Online website.

Get to Work Book (n.d.) is a popular planner and includes both a calendar and the equivalent of a task manager throughout its pages. The designers include motivational quotes that may be torn out of the book and hung on a wall. They provide a framework for reflecting on how to break down larger projects into smaller actions. Their home page asserts "Big Things Happen One Day at a Time," and they have designed a system to help break larger goals into the steps it will take to accomplish them.

On episode 237 of Teaching in Higher Ed, Rashida Crutchfield (2018) recommended a planner that former students of hers created and built a business around. I purchased a Passion Planner in early 2019 and am already enjoying having a tangible tool to use in certain circumstances. During meetings, I prefer not to use digital devices, lest I seem like my attention is not on the critical issues being discussed. Having the Passion Planner with me allows me to catch a glimpse of the big-picture calendar items, such as when I will be out of town or when significant events are occurring. If I need more detail on my schedule during the meeting, I can always reference the digital calendar on my smartphone. I capture action items from meetings in the Passion Planner and then add them into my digital task manager as follow-up. Their methodology allows me to identify the week's focus as well as good things that happened, and it even has what they refer to as a "space of infinite possibility," or a blank space to be used for any purpose (Passion Planner, n.d.).

In choosing which analog planner to use, it helps to think about the primary function you want it to fulfill. Some planners are less task managers and more oriented toward sketching or memory keeping. I like the opportunities for reflection built into many printed planners but prefer to have only high-level calendar items recorded in printed form because my schedule changes so frequently and would otherwise too quickly get out of date. Visit thriveonlineseries.com to view recommended analog task managers.

Invitation to Connect

Already have a favorite analog task manager/planner? Share your thoughts using #ThriveOnline.

Digital Task Management Systems

My digital task management application is one of the most essential components of my trusted system. When I open the program on my computer or phone, it has a calming effect on me. I am confident that what needs to get done is either all captured in there or about to be recorded.

My various roles are represented in folders in my task management program (see Figure 1.5):

- Mother, spouse, daughter, family member, friend
- Podcast producer and blogger
- Dean of teaching and learning
- Teacher (associate professor of business and management and adjunct professor of educational leadership)
- Writer/researcher
- Speaker

Figure 1.5. Folders representing various roles.

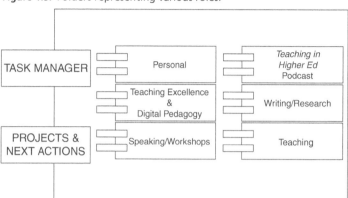

Under the teaching folder are projects for each class I am teaching in a given term:

- Teach: MGMT470
- Teach: EDD703

Under each class's project are all the next actions associated with it. I can tell how much grading I have left to do for a given course. There is an indication that I need to go back and make some modifications to an online class I just finished teaching. I am also reminded of my desire to consider inviting a guest speaker to participate in a synchronous session for my class in a few weeks.

Any follow-up on podcast episodes that have recently published is articulated as a task, along with a reminder to schedule upcoming social media posts. All my upcoming speaking engagements are listed as projects:

- Present: Retrieval Practice workshop at PTL
- Present: Delivering Dynamic Presentations at ACI
- Present: [to be determined] at DTE/CHE

For each of the presentations, I can make sure I am following up with the mundane but important steps related to being reimbursed for my expenses and paid for my work. I also include the necessary actions I will need to take to research for the talk, create the slide deck, and build a resources page on my website.

Another section of my task manager has a list of all items requiring follow-up from other people: Has John tested out the new feature in our LMS yet? Have I heard back from Cathy on whether she is up for being on the podcast this month? Has my mom replied about picking the kids up from school while we attend the podcasting conference next month? Did the help desk get back to me on whether we can integrate the new tool within our LMS?

I can easily pull up a list of things I need to talk to my husband about: Can he pick the kids up from school next Friday, since I need to stay on campus later than usual that day? How should we respond to the invitation for dinner with our friends who are coming to town? Should we schedule an extra date night to see a movie that keeps catching my eye? Could he order more floss for the kids?

My digital task management system is far better at holding all of these things than my brain ever could be. It helps me plan, execute, and follow up on the aspects of my life (including my teaching) that are most vital to making me feel like I am having an impact. I use this tool multiple times a day. It is essential to my sense of personal productivity and accomplishment.

Selecting a Digital Task Management System
The process of choosing a digital task management system can be overwhelming. Something you can do to ease that process is to identify what features are essential in making the tool work most effectively for you. At the top of the list will be whether or not the system is compatible with the devices that you use. If you are on a PC and have an Android phone, then the task manager you use needs to work on those two platforms.

Ease of use is another important consideration. I like to be able to get up and running fairly easy, but I also like when a tool has more advanced features so that as my knowledge about the system grows I can use those, too.

An essential feature for me in a task management system is the ability to set up a special email address such that I can send next actions to my task management system from within my email application. Some email applications integrate directly with specific task management systems, making it unnecessary to take the extra step of sending an email. The added advantage of this approach is that the location of the email is stored along with the task, making it easier to bring the email back up when working on it within the task manager.

Using a Task Manager
Visit thriveonlineseries.com to review recommended digital task managers. They have varied features, but all

have one common attribute: They are easy to learn to use. They let us get started using them quickly. Then, as we become more familiar with the basics, we can experiment with some of the more advanced features. Here is some guidance for using a task manager toward greater productivity:

- Use an action-oriented verb at the beginning of each task (e.g., Call: Juan regarding the Zoom license; Revise: Consumer behavior chapter 4 slide deck; Review: Conference possibilities for coming academic year; Capture: Action items from the last faculty development committee meeting).
- Group tasks under their related projects (e.g., Prep: MGMT470-2020f; Attend: Instructure conference; Rollout: Arc Media; Redesign: TiHE Website).
- Group one-off tasks that are not part of a specific project under a grouping named after the role to which they relate. I put these groupings in square brackets, so it is easier for me to distinguish them from the task groupings that are related to projects (e.g., [VU-Admin]; [Maintenance]; [Family-Admin]; [TiHE Admin]; [Personal-Admin]).
- Avoid putting due dates on tasks that are not actually due on a specific day. Instead, regularly schedule weekly and other reviews and determine what tasks to focus on during a given week using a feature like placing a flag on a task.

The most important aspect of any task manager, whether analog or digital, is that it travels with us wherever we go. If our analog task manager (planner) is not with us when we commit to take action, we run the risk of forgetting those next steps before they need to be completed. If we have access only to our digital task manager when we are at our computer, it is unlikely that we will be able to recall all the action items that we have encountered since the last time we sat at our desk.

MAXIMIZING THE USE OF CALENDARS

Most of us have kept a calendar at least since college, if not earlier. The key is that our calendar is with us at all times, whether composed on paper or tracked electronically on our computer and smartphone. Proactively looking at how we spend our time helps us be more productive. This section provides guidance on how to construct and use an ideal week calendar, as well as what to keep on your primary calendar.

Ideal Week Calendar

Reflecting on how we would ideally like to spend our time each week can give us a metric to use when comparing how we actually invested our time. "You have a choice in life. You can either live on purpose, according to a plan you've set. You can live by accident, reacting to the demands of others. The first approach is proactive; the second reactive," asserts Hyatt (2011, para. 1), former CEO of Thomas Nelson Publishers and current writer, speaker, and coach. He uses a more proactive approach in thinking about his schedule by designing an ideal week.

Hyatt explains, "My Ideal Week—the week I would live if I could control 100% of what happens—is divided into a simple grid. Each day has a theme. In addition, each day is segmented according to a specific focus area" (para. 5).

This is how Hyatt blocks out each day of his week: Mondays are dedicated to tasks related to the team he manages. Tuesdays and Wednesdays are times to travel, or for longer meetings. Thursdays are more open for what external meeting requests might need to be scheduled. Fridays are devoted to planning and reflection. Saturdays are focused on more personal work and events. Finally, Sundays are reserved for church, relaxation, and being sure to take time out to plan the following week.

Next, he blocks out certain hours of each day to reflect his circadian rhythms and preferences. Hyatt has a focus area every day that has his "early morning hours devoted to self: reading, praying, and working out" (para. 7). The middle portions of his days are dedicated to work-related activities. Finally, he ends each day with time with his family and with writing.

I have adopted his methodology to fit my typical weeks a bit better, given that I have big swings in what my weekdays might look like, depending on whether I am teaching. For example, on days when I am teaching, it does not work for me to exercise before I head off to my institution. Instead, I can schedule a block of time in the middle of the afternoon to take a 30-minute walk around our campus. Incidentally, this block for walking is often an excellent time to catch up with a colleague, instead of doing that in a more solitary setting, like I used to.

Since 2012, when I was introduced to the idea, I have been creating an ideal week every semester with one exception, when my job changed at my institution. It took some time for me to get a sense of the rhythms of the new role. I went from teaching four classes every semester and having teaching as my primary function to teaching one class each semester and having faculty development as my main focus. At first, it felt like a 24/7 job. Faculty work nontraditional hours, but I fell into the temptation of thinking I needed to be there to "save the day" at all hours.

As I learned more about how to make my experience in the role more sustainable and to be able to serve my faculty colleagues in not only the urgent things but also longer term foci, I found that having an ideal week template helped to guide me. I was able to think through what is most important to me and how to be sure to structure my schedule each week to reflect those priorities. You can learn more about Hyatt's ideal week system and get a link to download his ideal week template on the book's website.

Primary Calendar Contents

While visiting the campus of Northwestern University in 1954, Dwight Eisenhower stated, "I have two kinds of problems, the urgent and the important. The urgent are not important, and the important are never urgent" (para. 17).

Eisenhower attributed the quote to a former college president and did not claim the words as his own.

However, the idea of breaking up our problems into ones that are urgent and important still wound up named after him as the "Eisenhower matrix" (see Figure 1.6)

It is wise to keep Eisenhower in mind when considering how we spend our time. It is easy to fall victim to the trap of focusing solely on those tasks that are screaming for attention. Our smartphones have been programmed to keep demanding our focus, through the default settings of notifications, drawing us in to check social media or email on our devices. The best places to invest our time are often in the things that are not urgent but are important.

Figure 1.6. Eisenhower matrix.

	URGENT	NOT URGENT
I M P O R T A N T	QUADRANT I	QUADRANT II
U N I M P O R T A N T	QUADRANT III	QUADRANT IV

Covey (2012) also proposed that we should make important distinctions when determining how to spend our time, echoing Eisenhower's remarks. The first dichotomy he said to explore is the difference between those tasks that are important and those that are unimportant. The latest season of a favorite television show, although certainly entertaining, is not considered important. However, a virtual conference with a student who is struggling with a course concept can be vital.

Covey also suggested identifying those tasks that are urgent and those that are not urgent. A synchronous session for an online course is urgent. It happens at a scheduled time. If we fail to facilitate the session, the opportunity to conduct that particular meeting will have come and gone. Responding to a student's email is not urgent. That does not mean that getting back to the student is unimportant, but rather that the reply does not have to happen at a specific time.

There are two schools of thought about what to put on your calendar. Allen (2015) is stringent about the calendar containing only actions that have to occur at a specific time and in a particular place (e.g., a physical location, using a phone, etc.). He recommends, "The calendar should show only the 'hard landscape' around which you do the rest of your actions" (p. 145).

The other approach for calendaring is to have everything listed using the same criteria as Allen's but then to add in blocks of time to allow for more focus on Quadrant II work. Having a couple of hours blocked out in an afternoon to focus on actions related to those things that are not urgent but are important can help us remain more accountable to this vital part of our work that hardly ever gets enough attention.

I find I am better able to maintain a system I can trust by initially placing only time-based commitments on my calendar. Then, once a week, I add time blocks into my week that will help represent the time I will need to focus on longer term priorities.

The goal is to have a productivity system that we trust. It should reflect our priorities and those actions that we have committed to taking. The following recommendations help build a trusted system:

- Enter due dates only for those tasks/actions that genuinely have a deadline by which they need to be completed.
- Conduct regular reviews. The process of regular reviews assists in keeping future commitments in the forefront.
- Assign a priority or flag to tasks in the task manager to provide a means for identifying those items that require our attention.

Remember, our calendars should be trustworthy, as well, and reflect only specific commitments we have made that need to occur at a particular time and in a designated place (including phone calls and virtual meetings). The method of strategically blocking times on our calendars to focus on high-priority actions can be helpful, yet those tasks should also be reflected within a task manager. Otherwise, the time we devoted to that action may go by without us completing it, and then it becomes all too easy to completely forget about needing to do it.

Accommodating Students Located in Different Time Zones

When teaching online students who live in different time zones, it can be challenging to navigate the best times to meet. Ideally, the programs we teach in will determine consistent, predetermined times to meet with our students for a given class. These expectations should be articulated in the academic schedules, as students determine which courses they will take and what will fit within their parameters.

However, there may be times when we still need to coordinate a time with students that crosses time zones as a part of our online teaching responsibilities. One person who navigates between time zones regularly is Maha Bali, one of the cofounders and codirectors of Virtually Connecting. This grassroots organization is a volunteer-based effort to "enliven virtual participation in academic conferences, widening access to a fuller conference experience for those who cannot be physically present at conferences" (Virtually Connecting, 2015, para. 1). Bali (2016) wrote for *The Chronicle of Higher Education*'s ProfHacker blog about two tools from World Time Buddy that she finds particularly helpful for what she calls the "timezone-challenged."

World Time Buddy
One useful way to plan online sessions with students is to use World Time Buddy, a time zone conversion and

calendaring tool. This service provides features that help coordinate meeting times with people who are geographically dispersed, options to schedule time in various ways, and plenty of customization options. The free service has limitations, such as serving up advertising, being able to view only four locations' time zones at a time, and not being able to link up what is shown on the mobile app with the account built on the website. If regularly teaching students in various time zones is part of an online teaching role, it may be worth considering one of their paid plans. The rest of what is described about World Time Buddy is possible with a free account unless otherwise specified.

The first step in leveraging the power of World Time Buddy is to enter the time zones in which students live to determine possible times that could be good for scheduling a synchronous class session or optional virtual meeting. The default length of meeting time is one hour, but that can be adjusted by selecting a longer duration.

Once a suitable time has been established, the meeting time can be added to a calendar invite (on Microsoft Outlook, Apple's iCal calendar format, or Google Calendar), or it can be copied to the clipboard for pasting or opened in an email using Gmail. Opening the event using this method allows for it to be saved within one's primary calendar.

However, it is important to get the word out to students, too. World Time Buddy has a widget that can be embedded within an LMS page or included on a website that reflects the event times to online students. The widget can determine where a given student is located and show the student the event time in local time, in addition to showing the professor's time zone. It can be configured to show not only the meeting date and time but also a countdown clock. Bali finds the widget especially useful when coordinating all the people it takes to make a successful Virtually Connecting event.

Other Time Zone Tools
The meeting planner feature of the website timeanddate .com can be helpful in locating possible times to meet. Worldtimeserver.com also has ways to see up to five locations at one time and save favorites. Finally, everytimezone .com has similar features that account for differing time zones when finding a time for online students to meet.

Invitation to Connect
What tools and techniques have you found helpful in scheduling with students who are located in different time zones? Share your thoughts using #ThriveOnline.

When to Make Assignments Due
Opinions range widely on the ideal time for making assignments due. On one hand, it is vital to consider the due dates and times from the students' perspectives, given the conflicting priorities that they so often have while pursuing higher education. On the other hand, it is helpful to consider the turn-around time that will be needed in order to promptly provide feedback, especially if future assignments will build on the current one.

If possible, have consistency for when assignments are due within an online program. When teaching undergraduate courses, I tend to have assignments due on Fridays before 5:00 p.m. This has helped reduce procrastination and the possibility of students completing work when they are in a state of exhaustion (which the midnight times tend to encourage). Because my doctoral students tend to need to do much of their coursework on the weekends, I typically have assignments due on Saturdays by midnight (because that time is the norm in the program, but ideally I would prefer an earlier time).

TAKE ACTION: TRANSLATING INTENTION INTO ACTION

This is an opportunity to reflect on which steps are most important to take after reading through Part One. Here are specific next actions you may want to record either in your task manager or in a someday/maybe list to increase the impact of the book:

❑ Reflect on the strengths and limitations of your current goal-setting approach. Then set some goals for the coming trimester, or whatever time boundaries best meet your needs.

❑ If you have not already selected a task manager, research some of the options and set it up to track all of the actions that need to be taken to move a project forward toward completion. While to-do lists can be paper based, you may find that an electronic one is more portable (because it can live on your computer and phone).

❑ Create an ideal week schedule for an upcoming term/semester.

❑ Set up your calendar so that it is always a current reflection of your time-based commitments and helps you reflect on how you are spending your time. Add calendar entries only for items that need to occur at a specific time. Or, if you decide to block off time to complete Quadrant II tasks, be sure to also still have that action recorded in your task manager.

❑ Identify tasks that are not urgent but are important and get them recorded in a task management system for follow-up.

❑ Set up the following other systems of organization, if you have not already done so: someday/maybe list, waiting-for list, and projects list.

❑ Change your pattern and avoid setting due dates for tasks/next actions that are not actually due on a particular day. Use priority indications or other means for bringing these items to your attention.

❑ Spend time evaluating your current suite of tools used in your productivity and distinguish which ones are meeting your needs and which ones may justify a replacement.

❑ Use #ThriveOnline and share what kind of task manager you either use or are planning on adopting.

❑ Visit the Thrive Online website at thriveonlineseries .com to discover other tools (digital and analog) that you may want to research.

PART TWO

FACILITATING COMMUNICATION

FACILITATING COMMUNICATION

Effective communication is a vital element of any class. Yet we often struggle to keep up with the quantity of email we receive, attending to students' requests to schedule a time to meet, and effectively communicating our expectations for assignments or answering learners' questions. There are methods we can use to streamline these processes, however, and free up more of our time for more meaningful communication. Being present is one of the best ways we can help our students achieve their goals and give them the feeling that there is someone supporting them along the way.

Some of our messages are directed at the entire class and may be made more efficient through techniques such as scheduling messages to be sent in advance. The interactions we have with individual students are paramount to effective teaching. As Sleeter (2014) emphasizes, "High-quality online education requires instructors to engage with students on an individual level rather than merely provide oversight as students proceed through the course" (para. 3).

It is worthwhile to invest time in communication because it can make such a difference in students' learning and in their experience in a class. Richardson and Swan (2003) found that students who perceive that they received good communication in a course are also more likely to self-report that they learned more in the class and were satisfied with their professor. When we make efforts toward facilitating communication in a course, students will take notice. Conversely, lack of interaction has been demonstrated to factor heavily in students' dissatisfaction in a course (e.g., Cole, Shelley, & Swartz, 2014).

Effective communication does take a lot of effort and time, however. How do we communicate effectively with our students while still being able to manage other priorities in our work? This section of *The Productive Online and Offline Professor* addresses email management, various alternative communication tools, and methods for greater communication available in LMSs.

EMAIL: CHALLENGES AND OPPORTUNITIES

It can be challenging to address a high volume of email, particularly given that online students are more likely to email professors than call them. We receive many different types of emails on any given day, each of which should be weighted differently. In this section, we consider several approaches to handling emails and the challenges that each approach produces. We then discuss strategies for how to minimize those difficulties. Let us begin by comparing what would happen if we treated our physical mailbox using the same approaches many of us use to navigate a high load of incoming emails.

Jon goes outside to see the mail he stores in his mailbox. He notices that his electric bill is overdue and that he has not remembered to RSVP for his cousin's wedding. Moving the thick stack of envelopes around, he attempts to see if anything else in there is urgent. His cousin will understand his late reply because Jon just finished a substantial grant proposal and had vented to his cousin about how extensive it was. His contract for the next academic year is taking up room in the mailbox. It can stay there because it is not due back signed for a few more weeks. The electric bill can wait until Monday, when Jon plans on paying other bills. Jon sighs and goes back inside, empty-handed. He will return to the mailbox in the coming week to sort through any urgent items.

It is easy to discern the absurdity of Jon's management of the mail in his mailbox. It is much harder to evaluate one's own downfalls when it comes to managing electronic mail. In the following sections, challenges encountered when using email and opportunities to negate or reduce those difficulties are explored.

Challenge: Using Email as a To-Do List

As emails arrive in our inboxes, they can sometimes represent actions that require follow-up. The trouble is that these messages are mixed in with others of far less importance. Also, these email-based task requests are isolated from the other priorities that we have. Using this method of email management can quickly lead to having thousands of emails in your inbox, with little idea of what to tackle next and the possibility of gaining a reputation of someone who lacks follow-through. Opening our mail applications can be a real source of stress because we know we can be confronted with an abundance of unfulfilled commitments or unanswered questions. It also means that we are allowing external factors to drive what gets our attention, versus reflecting on what is most important to attend to.

Our online students need to hear from us regularly for them to recognize that we are here to support them in their learning. If our inboxes get out of control, our students' questions can go unanswered. There is a better way of managing email that lets us take action on those messages that require our attention and remove from our focus those that do not.

Opportunity: Aim for Inbox Zero

Merlin Mann, an independent writer, speaker, and broadcaster, coined the phrase *inbox zero* to describe the ideal state of any inbox: empty. The phrase *inbox zero* usually refers to an empty email inbox but could also describe an empty inbox sitting on our desk. Mann gave an inbox zero talk at Google's headquarters in July of 2007, which is still referenced today. He conveyed the absurdity of handling our email messages differently than we would a physical mailbox. Jon's story at the beginning of this section is based loosely on Mann's description of a fictitious way of handling our physical mail in his talk.

Mann (2007) asserts that every email represents a decision. Each email's decision can be broken down into the following six categories:

1. *Delete*: Get rid of it. Quickly.
2. *Delegate*: Pass the action on to someone else who is better able to address it.
3. *Respond*: Reply to the person and the request if it requires only a quick answer.
4. *Defer*: If the action is going to take more than two minutes to complete, move it over to a task manager and move the email out of the inbox. Having the next action in a task manager allows it to be viewed in the context of other priorities that have been identified within that trusted system.
5. *Do*: If the task's completion can be met in less than two minutes, take care of it right now. Otherwise, get it moved over to a task manager.
6. *Archive*: If the information contained in the email is likely to need to be referenced at a later date, move the email out of the inbox and into an archive folder.

Once every email in an inbox has been processed with these six decision points in mind, it will be empty. The resulting unoccupied inbox is known as inbox zero in Mann's (2007) vernacular. All commitments have been properly captured, and superfluous emails will not take up precious time and attention. When inbox zero has been achieved, it does not mean that all of the action items represented in the emails are complete. Instead, we have trashed messages that did not require our attention and are not needed for future reference, archived messages that we may need to refer to at some point, or transferred the actions from email to a task manager. Storing the actions that were represented by the emails within our task manager allows us to prioritize more effectively how these tasks fit in with the other things we have on our plate.

Challenge: Inbox Overflow

The concept of inbox zero can be daunting to think about. Someone who has allowed their inbox to accumulate and has more than 5,000 emails in there is going to have a hard time envisioning what it would be like to achieve inbox zero once a day. With each new important email that arrives, the fear increases that one of the thousands of messages already in the inbox might turn out to be vital but will be tucked too far out of the way to gain attention. It is impossible to be aware of that many potential actions requiring our attention as long as messages continue to build up.

Opportunity: Perform an Email "Reset" by Archiving All Messages in the Inbox

The first step to achieving a more manageable email inbox is recognizing that email clients make terrible task managers. It is all too easy to reread the same messages repeatedly. Each time we look at an email more than once, it takes valuable processing time and mental energy to rethink how we might address the content of that email. Email clients are suitable for receiving messages, replying

When inbox zero has been achieved, it does not mean that all of the action items represented in the emails are complete.

#ThriveOnline

to messages, and storing older messages in case they need to be referenced later on.

There are two ways to set up an email reference system. The first method is to tuck away all messages in a single archive folder. This method allows for the inbox to include only recent, incoming messages. The archive folder contains all the past emails which can be accessed for future reference by searching for the sender, the subject line, the date sent, or even the contents of the email.

The second method for setting up an email reference system is to use folders. It is best to set up as few folders as needed, to minimize the amount of time required to locate a folder. Having as few folders as possible becomes especially important when managing email on a mobile device. Because the search capabilities of email clients are so powerful, most people stick with an archive folder and avoid worrying about managing multiple folders. However, if we have grown accustomed to organizing our emails in folders, it is not necessary to build a different habit if the current system is working.

The most important step to take in establishing a manageable email inbox is to perform an email "reset" by archiving all inbox messages into an archive folder. Many email clients already have a built-in archive folder. Create one, if necessary. Then, go back to the inbox and select all the messages that are located within it. (Control-a on Windows or command-a on a Mac chooses all the messages, without having to scroll.) Finally, drag the selected messages over to the archive folder, clearing out your inbox to now better serve its intended purpose.

Yes, it is possible that your email "reset" will mean that emails requiring follow-up are out of sight and easy to forget about. However, when our inboxes get unmanageable, it is not like we are able to manage the follow-up effectively using our approach of email inbox as task manager. Doing an email reset will mean the same downside of keeping an unmanageable amount of email in an inbox but will have the upside of being able to use email for its intended purpose going forward.

If conducting an email reset sounds daunting, try setting aside a few hours to capture all the tasks that are outlined within the emails that are currently in the inbox. Then move all emails into an archive or a folder, as previously described. If three hours is not sufficient, it may be time to recognize that the number of emails currently in an inbox is unmanageable and go for inbox zero. Keep in mind that all the emails that have been moved are still there in your email application. They just are not now fighting for our time and attention like the new ones that arrive are.

Challenge: Students Emailing With Questions They Should Know the Answers To

Given the time we often put into creating detailed syllabi and other course resources, it can be frustrating to receive questions from students that could be answered by a more thorough perusal of those materials. While we want students to take responsibility for their learning, we also want students to know that we are here to support them in the process.

It can be helpful to remember just how overwhelming it can be to start a new educational journey, whether transitioning from high school to college or going back to school after 20 years without any formal education. Empathy can go a long way toward bridging the gap between a desire for students to have greater self-reliance and their need for coaching and help during a big transition.

Opportunity: Make Conversations More Public

The response to a student's query about an upcoming assignment can be forwarded to the entire course in an announcement to reduce the likelihood of receiving other emails with the same question in the future. Regardless of whether students receive direct answers from their professor on how to locate the answers to their questions, it is helpful to open question answering to more than just the person teaching the class.

A discussion board forum may be devoted to questions and answers. Students should be encouraged to participate in providing guidance to other learners. We can still provide additional clarification when needed but having more of a sense of community makes for a better learning experience and requires less of our time. It is best to avoid being the first person who answers each question on this forum because students may perceive that their involvement is not wanted or needed.

It is a good investment of time to track the kinds of questions that arise at various points in the class. Consider how the syllabus might be modified to better address the queries that are received. I tend to think about just-in-time information that can be provided to students within the LMS—right at the moment when they are beginning work on an assignment. I make sure to provide answers to the following questions for each assignment directly as it is introduced to students:

- What is the purpose of the assignment? How will it support the students' learning and in what ways does it align with the course learning outcomes?
- When is it due, and what type of artifact will be submitted (e.g., paper, video)?
- How will the assignment be graded? (I link to a rubric, at this point, if one is used for the assignment.)

Including information in a consistent way throughout the class helps reduce the questions students have (and therefore reduces my email load). I regularly modify the information in my syllabi and course assignments to continually improve communication to my students over time.

Another helpful tool to have is a screencasting application. These services record what is happening on our screen and can also include a recording of our voices as we share our answers to student questions. I use a lightweight sharing app called Droplr. It allows me to quickly record a short video showing how to do something. As soon as I stop the recording, a link to the video is copied to my clipboard. Then, when I press command-v (on a Mac) or Ctrl-v (on Windows), the link is pasted into my response. Droplr also has options to capture screenshots (pictures of what is on the screen) that can be annotated and also gives the opportunity to record a GIF (a short video that does not contain sound). Students regularly tell me how much easier it is to understand things when I share these short screencast videos with them, and I absolutely love how quickly I can respond, especially given that I do not have to worry about uploading the video and generating a link to send.

Challenge: Online Students Are in Differing Time Zones and Keep Varied Schedules

Students cite a desire for flexibility in their educational pursuits as a primary driver in the demand for online learning. Although most online students wind up being within 100 miles of the campus they choose for their online courses, there are still plenty of people taking coursework from around the world.

Most students need to work while taking online courses, which adds to the complexity of attempting to respond to email during the times when students need answers urgently. None of us wants to be checking email 24/7. The exploration of a tool that can more effectively address these kinds of needs, therefore, becomes that much more important.

Opportunity: Use an Email Alternative, Such as Slack

When email was first released, it was a novel way to communicate that was far superior to sending something through the post office. Today, the convenience of email

Students cite a desire for flexibility in their educational pursuits as a primary driver in the demand for online learning.

#ThriveOnline

has been surpassed by the feeling that we're drowning in it. Email alternatives, such as Slack, take the best of what email has to offer while attempting to rid us of some of the real downsides.

Slack is what happens when email, instant messaging, and file sharing all get combined into a single tool. Following are the three most vital features of Slack's success:

1. *Search*: Slack makes it easy to find what a user is looking for, whether a file that has been uploaded to the system or a conversation thread from months ago about a course change.
2. *Synchronization*: No matter what method is being used to access Slack (a smartphone app, the web, the Slack application, or a tablet), Slack remembers where someone left off. Messages that have already been viewed are marked as read, and only new interactions are brought to the forefront.
3. *Simple file sharing*: Images can be copied/pasted into Slack with ease, or a file can be dragged and dropped directly into the app.

Some faculty are experimenting with using Slack as an LMS replacement or an enhancement to the traditional LMS framework. Robert Talbert (personal communication) explains that he has divided the work of various tools as follows: Anything that has a grade associated with it goes in the LMS, files all go inside Google Drive, and everything else goes in Slack.

Steven Michels (2016) of Sacred Heart University shared on his YouTube channel how he taught two of his online courses using Slack. He stresses how simple using

Slack is and how easy it is for professors and students to engage with one another. His theory is that Slack is like one big, gorgeous discussion board.

Slack channels can be created to organize the information being discussed into different topics. Michels (2016) set up numbered channels to keep his course structure transparent. A Slack administrator can allow users to add their own channels, but Michels kept channel creation powers in his hands, thus ensuring the overall goal of making items easy to find. For more information, a link to Michels's video may be found on thriveonlineseries.com.

Michels (2016) stresses the importance of the immediacy of Slack versus email and other notifications that come from an LMS. He described how the morning after a tragedy had occurred he decided to get in touch with his students via Slack to see how they were doing. He reported that many students were live on Slack and able to share their reflections about what had happened. The ability to connect live in such an impromptu way highlighted one of Slack's strengths.

That particular strength of Slack can also be a weakness. The way in which Slack makes communication easier can also mean that a flurry of messages can come within the various channels. Michels (2016) recommends thinking about what boundaries to set for yourself when teaching an online class using Slack. He suggests using the do not disturb features to keep your attention from being taken away from other priorities. It is also helpful to think carefully about the notification settings, so nudges to take a look at the conversations happening on Slack show up only in the situations that match your preferences.

Challenge: Regardless of Their Importance, All Emails Come to the Same Place

Another prevalent problem in using email is that all messages, regardless of their relative importance, come into the same inbox. Some email clients, such as Gmail and Microsoft Office 365, are attempting to negate this downside by doing some presorting for us.

Gmail's Priority Inbox includes a feature that sorts emails as important, unread, and all the rest. You can set up filters that create even greater granularity. A 20% off promotion can be set to arrive in an ancillary folder, hopefully leaving our attention to remain focused on more important messages.

Microsoft Office 365 has a similar feature, called "clutter," that moves messages that do not seem as important to us into a folder separate from our inbox. Over time, if Office 365 notices that we never open emails from a particular address or we quickly delete them, it routes new emails from that sender into the clutter folder. We can train messages to go into the right folder by dragging emails into the folder we would prefer they arrive in.

Opportunity: Use an Email Management Service, Such as SaneBox

Although Gmail and Microsoft are doing their part in attempting to make our inbox contain higher priority items, there are services out there that are further down the path in this endeavor. Determining whether or not to use such a service will require a couple of considerations. First, these services come at a cost. Evaluating the time saved versus the money spent will be an important consideration. Second, using one of these applications will likely require some security risk.

In order for a third party to parse out unimportant emails, access to your email is required. Some companies sort through email within their application. That means that this specific application will need to be running for emails to successfully be filtered. Other services intervene before the emails ever arrive in your inbox (or different folder) within your email application. Therefore, they need to have your email username and password to work their magic.

Although other companies are doing similar work that may be worth including in any decision on what email management service to use, as of this writing, SaneBox offers the most comprehensive features at a reasonable price. SaneBox works similarly to the tools from Google and Microsoft except that it contains even more features for making our email management less time intensive and more effective. For a current list of recommended services, see thriveonlineseries.com.

Once SaneBox is configured with your email account information and what features you want to use, it begins sorting your email into a number of different folders that then show up in whatever email client is being used. The @SaneLater folder contains emails that are deemed to be less crucial than the ones that would typically show up in the inbox. SaneBox is remarkably good at determining which emails belong in which folders. However, if it ever gets it wrong, simply dragging the email a single time into the preferred folder will "train" it to always show up in that same spot. Other Sane Box folders may be used to boost the power of SaneBox even more. I use the Sane-BlackHole folder to tell the service to never send me emails from that address again.

The time that is saved for each user on SaneBox gets tracked and reported back in a periodic email. If desired, users can compare their own utilization of the service to that of other SaneBox users they know. Services such as SaneBox offer one other way to spend less time on email, while still having a trusted service that brings the most important messages to the forefront.

Challenge: Students May Expect a Faster Reply Than You Require of Yourself

It is easy to become frustrated with or poke fun at students who seem to require an email response immediately after it has been sent. However, we should offer a healthy dose of empathy in this situation. Whenever any of us are struggling it helps to know at least what support we can expect when attempting to get unstuck.

Opportunity: Communicate Your Email Response Times

How we respond to students' email queries can send a message about our level of care for their learning. Immediacy is not the goal. These kinds of response times are not realistic in the vast majority of learning environments and can contribute to burnout. The goal should be to respond with empathy and to have set the stage early in a course regarding email response times.

Chickering and Gamson's (1999) research stresses the need for students to receive prompt feedback. Although not all student feedback needs to be channeled through email, students do tend to request help in this way, especially early in their work on unfamiliar assignments. Response times should be articulated in the syllabus and emphasized throughout the start of a class. I typically share with students that I try to be offline on Sundays, in order to keep my focus on my family. However, because many online learners need to invest time over the weekends to complete their coursework, I let them know that I will check email on Saturday afternoons and get back to them at that time.

In advance of teaching an online course, it is beneficial to think about email response times and how frequently email will be checked. The Walker Center for Teaching and Learning at the University of Tennessee at Chattanooga (n.d.) recommends considering using scheduled chats with students to capture questions and provide feedback in a more targeted way than email typically allows. Those chats can take place using the chat feature within an LMS or using a service that can offer chatlike features, such as Twitter. Of course, this is beneficial only when teaching students in the same or nearby time zones.

Invitation to Connect

Share your experiences with setting boundaries about how often you will check and respond to email using #ThriveOnline.

EMAIL TEMPLATES

The goal of increased efficiency is to have more time to be present for our students and all the other people who are important to us in our lives. That is vital to being someone who supports students in their learning. However, there will frequently be interactions with students that are more transactional than acting as mentors and coaches for them.

When we respond to these more transactional emails, we can fall into one of two categories: first, reiterating to students information that has already been communicated in other ways (e.g., the course syllabus, in our prior emails or announcements), and, second, refusing to answer their questions because the information can be found elsewhere, or we otherwise do not see it as our role to assist them with their query.

Instead of choosing one of those two extremes we can fall somewhere in the middle. We can empower students to have a better appreciation for what is available to them in the course or other materials. Additionally, we can reinforce that we are here to support them in what can often be an overwhelming process of learning to navigate higher education (whether they just graduated from high school or have not taken a course in years).

Email templates can help address the more transactional emails, which then frees our time for more meaningful communication with students. Schmitz (2013) stresses, "If you feel like you're typing the same emails frequently, it's time to streamline this. There's no point in typing the same emails over and over again" (para 22).

Email templates can help in answering frequent questions and requests.

Frequent Questions and Requests

Consider questions you frequently receive while teaching an online course. Perhaps the following are familiar:

- Your office hours/ways to get additional assistance
- Requests for letters of recommendation
- Your discipline (in my case, a student who is thinking about starting a business and wants to know how to explore ideas)
- When an assignment is due, or more clarification on how to approach getting started with it
- General questions about grades

Frustration can easily set in when you find that students are asking questions that you have already provided answers to. Instead, think of the benefits of creating a climate in your course where students feel that you are supporting them in their learning. What a student is inquiring about may not relate to your goals of mentoring her to get into her preferred graduate program, but it could be a small step toward building trust that eventually gets the two of you to that point down the road.

At the same time, do not waste your time on the less important task of providing information that could be found elsewhere. By creating a series of templates for emails that you commonly send, you free up your time to connect with your students in more meaningful ways.

Redirect Back to Resources

Rather than stating that something can be found under week 2 of your online course, use a link that takes students directly to that spot. Yes, it does take a bit more time to provide a link, instead of just typing that information to send the students back into the course, but I find that using the link means that I take the opportunity to make sure I am sending the person to the correct place. Plus, this allows me to reassess my own course navigation choices, to see if I have made things confusing by how I have structured that portion of the course.

Err on the Side of Kindness

It is easy to forget how intimidating we can be as professors. We can also lack empathy in recalling the difficulty of going back to school or starting a new program that is structured entirely different from anything we have yet to encounter in our educational experiences. When structuring email reply templates, build kindness into the process. Instead of the shaming approach ("I already provided you with that information in the syllabus"), you can alter that a bit and write something like the following:

> That information may be found in the syllabus [provide link]. There's a lot of information in there that will help you achieve your goals in this course, so take another look at it this week. Specifically, the details regarding that assignment are on page 8. I am glad you are already thinking ahead to the weeks to come. See you online this week.

Think of the benefits of creating a climate in your course where students feel that you are supporting them in their learning.

#ThriveOnline

Saving and Accessing Email Templates

There are plenty of places you might store your email templates. You could have them in Microsoft Word, for example, but I would recommend against that. Most important, you would have to open up Microsoft Word to access them and then copy/paste them into your email program. Also, Microsoft Word is notorious for having additional hidden formatting that you cannot see in your text but can create issues when pasting in an HTML editor, which some email clients have for composing emails. Even if that is not going to be an issue for the email client you use, there are still better options available.

Email Drafts Folder

Whether you use Outlook, Gmail, or another email client, there is a folder for drafts that is used to hold on to emails as you are composing them. If your email client crashes while you're writing an email, you usually can go back in and find it stored in the drafts folder/section of the email client.

If you use a smartphone or tablet for composing emails, or you have more than one computer, it may be worth setting up your various email clients/applications to all use the same drafts folder. If you start writing an email on your smartphone and you are not quite finished, you can always save it to your drafts and pick it back up later when you are working on your computer. While the process to accomplish this varies, typically, as you start to close the email, your email client/application will ask if you want to save it as a draft.

Although I make use of drafts for specific emails that I am working on, I do not typically use it for templates that I know I will use multiple times down the road. The email clients I use do not allow for enough organization to leverage drafts as much as I might like for templates. Instead, I use an application type known as text expansion.

Text Expansion Application

A text expansion program allows you to keep as many email templates (among other things) as you want for reuse down the road. The most popular text expansion application as of this writing is called TextExpander and is available on both Mac and Windows operating systems. You can organize email templates within TextExpander by class or by function in folders. Then, when you're ready to use one of them, you just type a few characters that you have predetermined will trigger an action to then "expand" into your full email template. This may be accomplished on a computer or on a mobile device.

If you have an email that you always send at the start of week 4, for example, you could use these characters as the trigger: ze-mailw4. As soon as you type in those characters, they will be replaced with the text from your email template. Part Four provides more information about text expansion applications as well as how to be more productive using TextExpander.

Notebook Application

Email templates can also be stored within a notebook or notes application. The advantage of this method is that the organizational structure of the program can be set up to our precise specifications. The disadvantage is that we have to open the application each time we are going to send one of these template emails, and then the specific email will need to be located.

Regardless of which method you choose for storing email templates, relocate them as your needs change. The important thing is to start building a database of email templates and to begin freeing up your time for more meaningful interaction with your students. It is also helpful to periodically go through the email templates you have developed and determine whether any course design adjustments can be made that would negate or reduce the need for some of them.

ONLINE SCHEDULING TOOLS

As we pursue greater productivity, we do not want it to be at the expense of being a resource for our students. Time for one-on-one communication is vital to the student experience, yet scheduling that time does not have to be cumbersome. We can use online scheduling tools to let us focus on the meaningful conversations we will have, instead of asking whether 1:00 p.m. works better than 2:00 p.m.

It is still hard for me to fathom how many educators in higher education are sitting in their offices, alone, for six to eight hours a week, waiting for a student to show up to their office hours. Those who teach online have needed to be more creative than that because we work with geographically distributed students. Given that a big motivator for students to take online courses is the flexibility it offers, it makes sense to take a different approach to office hours.

While email is a common way for online students to ask questions of their professors, it is still good practice to have designated times each week when students know you will be available to communicate with them. However, to ensure that you are prepared to address a learner's needs, I suggest using an online scheduling service.

Core Features

The competitive landscape of online scheduling tools is vast. A new tool comes into the mix regularly, leapfrogging existing companies' feature set. While it is easy to be lured by the latest entrant, we also want to do our best to stick with a company that is most likely to be around for a while because the firm has a sustainable business model.

I have used a few of these different services. See thriveonlineseries.com for a current list of recommended online scheduling services. The fundamental features of any scheduling tool I would use needs to include the following:

- *Different appointment types*: Any tool that will be sufficient for serving the purpose of offering office hours sign-ups for students needs to possess the option to establish various appointment durations. One student may need only 15 minutes for his question, while another may a require an hour for an in-depth career direction discussion.

- *Appointment blocks*: Some calendaring tools open up your schedule way more than I am comfortable with. You may not have an actual appointment booked in your schedule at 8:00 a.m. on a Friday morning, but you may not want to list that among the options that are offered to students who are looking to connect with you. Instead, many of the services let you predetermine blocks of time that will be made available to students seeking to sign up for appointments with you, just like with more traditional office hours.

- *Compatibility with your preferred calendar application*: Whatever scheduling tool you select needs to be compatible with the calendar application you use. If you are on a Mac, and you use the built-in calendar, look for a system that offers iCal. Gmail users will want to have Google Calendar compatibility, while Windows users often use Outlook (Microsoft's email and calendaring application).

- *Calendar syncing*: After having set up a few appointment blocks that show your office hours availability, you may have something unexpected come up during that time. If you are going to attend your daughter's final soccer match during a time that would otherwise have been offered as a possibility for an office hours appointment, you can put the game in your calendar and have the appointment sync over to your scheduling tool. All appointments placed on your calendar during the appointment blocks you have established for office hours will show you as unavailable during those times. Office hours appointments that are booked on the scheduling service are then blocked off on your primary calendar, so you do not have to worry about placing another appointment on top of that already scheduled time. Regular syncing between a scheduling service and one's calendar makes for the most efficient means for addressing both needs.

- *Recurring appointments*: Given that most of your weeks will have similar patterns, it makes sense to keep consistent office hours availability. The feature of recurring appointments is, therefore, a big time saver. You can still make exceptions to those days/ times that do not fit the initial pattern that you have set up, but being able to repeat the same office hours and then determine where the exceptions are is an essential feature for a scheduling service.
- *Communication back to the person scheduling the appointment*: An email with a calendar invite confirming the time that has been scheduled is sent back to the person who scheduled the appointment.

Any scheduling service that has the preceding features will help support a professor's productivity. Next, let us explore how to set up a scheduling tool to meet your needs.

Recommended Process

When first setting up your office hours availability on a given service, determine what requirements your institution has regarding the number of hours or days offered. Often, universities will require one to two office hours for each course taught. Some also require that those hours be dispersed over a few different days.

After you have figured out what is required, consider what you know about your students' needs. If you have worked with this program's population of students previously, you likely know what the majority of their work lives may be like, though, of course, there are huge variations when teaching any group of learners.

I teach a couple of times a year in a doctoral program that has teachers, school principals, higher education managers/directors, and others who work in an educational context. Most of them work during the day and attend to family needs during the early evening hours. Offering some office hours during a traditional lunchtime, in the late afternoon, and at 7:30 p.m. means that I can support their diverse needs.

It is also helpful to think about what other scheduled aspects of a given course you may be able to tap into to offer office hours immediately before or after an event. In the case of the doctoral program, we have synchronous sessions every other week from 7:30 p.m. to 8:20 p.m. I open up my availability from 7:00 p.m. to 7:30 p.m. and from 8:20 p.m. to 8:50 p.m. on those same nights, which is ultimately more efficient for me and tends to work better for the students as well.

Some of the calendaring services let the users select the duration of time they prefer while they are setting up their time. Other scheduling tools have you set up different time blocks while you are setting up your office hours availability. I have grown accustomed to setting up separate appointment blocks (e.g., 15-minute, 30-minute, 45-minute), so students can request the amount of time they prefer.

See the online resources for this book at thrive onlineseries.com to find out what my current calendaring service of choice is, along with others I recommend checking out. Once you have set up your calendaring service, get ready to spend a lot less time emailing back and forth with students or waiting in front of an empty virtual office with no one showing up to your office hours. My calendar service is set up to automatically email students a reminder of our meeting one day in advance. Also, because they do not have to show up at an office, they can more easily fit joining me via web conferencing on their mobile device wherever they happen to be.

TEXT-BASED COMMUNICATION SERVICES

Texting is an easy means of communicating and one that is familiar to students. However, it can be challenging to determine whether to share one's cell phone number with students. Some faculty would rather not have the potential disruptions during nonworking days. It can be helpful to have some boundaries around when we are available to support students in their learning and when we are recharging our own batteries. If we rely on text messages as a means of communication, it can also be challenging to remember to go back and reply to a student's message if you decide to delay responding right away.

Fortunately, some services allow you to communicate with students via their cell phones without needing to accept the downsides of distributing a personal mobile number. Instead of trying to make your built-in text message service meet the needs of supporting learners in an online course, you can make use of services that were designed from their core to address your concerns and help your students succeed.

Remind

In this section, I share how I use a service called Remind. The online resources site for the book will be updated with any new recommendations I have for this type of service. Remind allows me to send a text message to all my students while keeping my cell number private. I can determine whether or not to let students reply to messages that I send out and can even create group messages to a smaller subset of students in a given class. Students' mobile numbers also remain private, though I have not really ever had a student who was apprehensive about providing me with that method of contact.

Students can receive Remind messages via their text message service on their cell phone, or they can download the Remind app. If they use the app, they have the small advantage of being able to respond with a reaction, meaning they can give your message a thumbs-up/thumbs-down, enter a question mark, or even give your message a round of applause.

Urgent Messages
What Remind does the best is provide an avenue for sending a critical message to an entire class without them also

Once you have set up your calendaring service, get ready to spend a lot less time emailing back and forth with students.

#ThriveOnline

receiving the professor's cell number. If you need to let students know that your online session is being held in a different virtual "place" than they are used to, you can fire up the Remind app on your smartphone or use the Remind website to send an announcement quickly and easily.

Reminder Messages

As evidenced by the name of the service, Remind is also well suited for sending reminder messages. If you have a scheduled online session coming up in a couple of days, you may want to send a reminder of the link students should use to join your online course event. You can also send a message 15 minutes ahead of the meeting time asking students to log in during the next few minutes to test their sound and make sure everything is working as expected. These reminders can be scheduled in advance to allow you to keep your mind focused on other things before your online sessions.

Some colleagues express frustration over needing to remind students of meetings that they should already have on their calendars. While I do think it is important for us to support our students in cultivating their time management skills, I can also say that the time it takes me to address an issue of a student forgetting about an online session is far more problematic for me than the perceived need to add a few more reminders into my online courses. I do not send reminders for everything in an online course, but I do send them for some of the more significant milestones. I tend to leverage Remind more for conveying information about upcoming synchronous sessions than I do for assignments that students are working on at their own pace.

Retrieval Practice

Instead of focusing as much on pouring information into our students' heads, retrieval practice gives our students the opportunity to practice getting knowledge back out of their heads (Agarwal, n.d.). Remind can be used to help students retain information through the process of retrieval practice, or helping students practice retrieving the information that is in their head and building stronger neural connections. Although Remind is not explicitly designed for quizzing, you can send a message to students with a fill-in-the-blank question or a multiple-choice inquiry. Most of my classes do not exceed 35 students, so I tend to let each student who replies know whether an answer was correct. With a more substantial number of students, you can send a follow-up message to the entire class an hour or two after having sent the initial message. Just be sure you do not wait too long before providing students with the correct answer, or you may negate the benefits of retrieval practice.

Encouragement

When I am grading assignments or exams, I often text students who have performed particularly well. This touchpoint reminds students that I am beside them during their journey throughout the course. It gives them an opportunity to hear of their success before even needing to log in to the LMS. If you are concerned about communicating a student's grade outside of the LMS, you can always send a text message congratulating the student and encouraging the student to log in to view the score when possible.

One-on-One Communication

Just like with a regular text message exchange, I can communicate back and forth with an individual student using Remind. The difference is that I can set up for these messages to be routed through the Remind app on my smartphone and can leave my preferred notification settings in place for non-teaching-related communication. In my case, I allow for a badge to show up on the app, indicating that someone has sent me a message on Remind, but I do not like to have each and every message coming through on my phone, as standard text messages do.

If I am in the middle of a communication-intensive time for a course, such as when we are about to conduct our first live online course session, I can modify the settings, temporarily, and receive more intrusive notifications. Then, when we shift back to more asynchronous interactions, I can switch the settings back to being aware of incoming messages only when I see the app's badge on my phone's home screen.

SYNCHRONOUS AND ASYNCHRONOUS VIDEO TOOLS

Being present for our online students can require more intentionality than face-to-face classes. The use of video can help us connect in ways that the written word may not afford us. We can engage with our students at a scheduled time (i.e., synchronous online learning) or have students watch, create, and share video in an unscheduled (asynchronous) way.

Most institutions have some form of synchronous communication technology available to those of us who teach online. It is worth finding out if your institution has such an arrangement because when all the professors are using the same tool for scheduled sessions it creates more consistency for the students. The book's website has a list of options, in case there is a need for evaluating which tool to use.

Office hours and other time to connect with students can be conducted using these kinds of tools as well. One particularly helpful feature that many of the videoconferencing tools have is the ability to share screens. My preferred synchronous technology is Zoom, which makes it incredibly easy for me to share whatever is on my screen, or to have students share their screens with me. I can show a slide deck this way or demonstrate where to locate something on the LMS. It makes answering students' questions a lot easier and gives them the sense that they have the support they need in their learning.

If you have predetermined synchronous sessions with your classes, determine whether your videoconferencing tool has the capability of scheduling repeated events. Zoom can schedule all class meetings at the same time, instead of requiring that each individual session be calendared.

There has been a significant increase in the use of asynchronous video in higher education courses in recent years (Borup, West, & Graham, 2013). Asynchronous video can have varied benefits, from supporting English language learners to providing greater flexibility for students who work and giving additional encouragement to students with low self-regulation as they proceed in a class.

The Thrive Online website (thriveonlineseries.com) is a useful way to explore synchronous and asynchronous video communication tools to realize some of these benefits in your teaching.

Invitation to Connect

Share what services you are finding more beneficial in facilitating synchronous and asynchronous communication in your teaching using #ThriveOnline.

LMS COMMUNICATION

Several communication tools are built into most LMSs. They can help us streamline our transmission of information to our students and develop a greater sense of connection with them.

Announcements allow us to communicate via email, while also posting the information in the LMS the next time students log in to the system. Saving the announcements that are sent is useful because you can then repurpose and resend them in future courses. These announcement-type messages can be stored in the same place as email templates, as described in an earlier section, to make them easier to locate in the future.

Video can be included in an announcement, making the communication that much richer. These types of videos are intended to be short and to the point; otherwise the time it would take to process an announcement in the course would become too long.

Links back to specific sections of the LMS can also be provided to direct students to the particular place where they can find additional information. If an assignment is due at the close of a week, consider linking directly to the site where students will need to submit it, or to a location within the LMS where they can find more information. The more we can get students engaged within the course structure that has been set up within the LMS, the more ease they will have navigating the course.

TAKE ACTION: FACILITATING COMMUNICATION

This is an opportunity to reflect on which steps are most important to take after reading through Part Two. Here are specific next actions you may want to record in your task manager or in a someday/maybe list to increase the impact of the book:

❑ Reflect on how you "show up" when teaching online courses. Consider any areas in which you could be more present for your students.

❑ Commit not to use an email client as a task manager. Instead, set up a task manager app that can track tasks and allows for a bigger picture perspective than when we look only at what is contained in our emails.

- ❏ Locate the unique email address for your preferred task manager and start emailing tasks directly to it from an email client.
- ❏ If you have a backlog of emails in your inbox, move all emails from the inbox into an archive folder and get a fresh start.
- ❏ Set up a means for conversations in online classes to become more public. This can take place by setting up a discussion board within the LMS or by using a third-party tool, such as Slack.
- ❏ Consider setting up an email management service, such as SaneBox.
- ❏ Include email response times and other expectations surrounding communication within your syllabus.
- ❏ Share using #ThriveOnline what tools you are finding particularly useful in facilitating communication with your students.
- ❏ Create and store a series of email templates to answer frequently asked questions. These messages may be stored in the drafts folder inside an email client, in a text expansion service, or in a notebook application.
- ❏ Determine core feature needs for an online scheduling tool and select the tool that best fits your needs.

- ❑ Identify whether a text-based communication service, such as Remind, might help streamline your communication with students and allow for greater control over how these kinds of interactions occur.
- ❑ Research whether your institution has a subscription to a synchronous videoconferencing tool and learn how to get started with it.
- ❑ Ensure that your tool kit includes a means for using asynchronous video in your teaching.
- ❑ Visit the Thrive Online website at thriveonlineseries .com to discover other tools that you may want to research.

PART THREE

FINDING, CURATING, AND SHARING KNOWLEDGE

FINDING, CURATING, AND SHARING KNOWLEDGE

Instead of being at the mercy of all the information that flies our way daily, we can discover a more proactive approach to finding, curating, and sharing knowledge. PKM allows us to find credible sources of information that we research or discover through a PLN. We can then transform that information into knowledge, so that it has some use for us either now or in the future. Finally, we can make meaning out of the knowledge and share it with others in our networked communities. PKM helps us be more productive by not reacting to the barrage of information coming from all directions and instead having a relevant and efficient means for discovering, making sense of, and sharing our learning.

Instead of having to scramble when we are developing a new course or are working on a project related to our field, we can use PKM to find, curate, and share information on an ongoing basis. By continually committing ourselves to this process of making sense of what we are taking in and finding ways to share that knowledge with our students and in our learning communities, we can be more productive for longer.

Most of us conducted a process resembling PKM as we pursued advanced degrees. We researched a topic that was relevant to our discipline; made sense of it by synthesizing what we read and analyzing the information through different lenses; and then shared our findings through some type of demonstration of our learning, such as writing a thesis or dissertation. Typically, the type of research we did was more solitary in nature or required collaboration with a small number of people. The type of PKM described here is broader than our academic research interests and contributes to our pursuit of lifelong learning.

Jarche (n.d.) defines *PKM* as a "set of processes, individually constructed, to help each of us make sense of our world, work more effectively, and contribute to society" (para. 1). Jarche (n.d.) uses the word *mastery* in place of the more commonly used word *management* because it is more descriptive of the aim of PKM. When we have personal mastery, we can make more sense of the complex organizations in which we work. Senge (2010) describes personal mastery as "the discipline of continually clarifying and deepening our personal vision, of focusing our energies, of developing patience, and of seeing reality objectively" (p. 7). We are aware of the gaps in our

A PKM system becomes personal when we include resources that will be relevant because of our strengths, our interests, and our motivations.

#ThriveOnline

knowledge and how we are pursuing lifelong learning using PKM.

Part Three explores the process of PKM and how we seek, sense, and share. It includes an example of how a faculty member teaching a new online course could use PKM to provide relevant and current knowledge.

PKM

The practice of personal knowledge management (or mastery) can be transformative in our ability to keep abreast of what is happening in our disciplines and in other areas of interest.

Personal

Part of the trouble with the overwhelming amount of information that flows our way daily is that it does not provide us with much value because it is not personal to us. Despite social media companies claiming to "personalize" advertisements that they direct our way, we all have examples of when their algorithms very poorly predicted what might be of interest to us.

A PKM system becomes personal when we include resources that will be relevant because of our strengths, our interests, and our motivations. Jarche (n.d.) stresses that a "personal" knowledge mastery system is "not directed by external forces" (para. 2). We create our PKM process by continually reflecting on what is most relevant for our current state and what is emerging as more important as we grow and develop in new areas.

Knowledge

Information is useless unless it is relevant to us or may be acted on in some way. Information is made up of data and context and can be easily reproduced. Knowledge is information that has become most useful to us and allows for learning to take place. We may not always know exactly what information will become beneficial to us in the future, which is one of the reasons why PKM is described as a process and not an end point. We might be assigned to teach a new class and all of a sudden have a keen interest in a topic that was not as relevant to us the day before.

Mastery

As we continually become more aware of who we are and who we are becoming, we are better able to make sense of information and determine its relevance to us. We become masters of our learning and continual movement toward our personal vision. According to Senge (2010), we never achieve our personal vision; instead, mastery functions as a way of bringing us closer to where we dream of being. He uses an analogy of a rubber band continually being stretched to pull us forward toward our vision.

PKM: SEEK, SENSE, SHARE

For most of us, reading a daily paper used to suffice as a means of acquiring the information we needed. However, Jarche (2014) articulates three external forces that are changing the way we work. First, technology is advancing such that more is possible than ever before. Second, we operate within the context of globalization, and this is changing how value gets created within companies. Third, social media allows for stronger and more effective learning networks to connect us. PKM enables us to become increasingly more effective at finding relevant information, making sense of it, and sharing it within communities (see Figure 3.1).

Seek

The process of seeking information can take place in two broad ways. First, we can be more purposeful in seeking

Figure 3.1. PKM model.

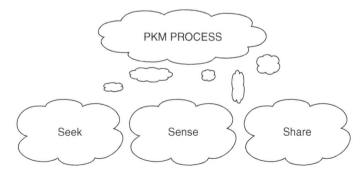

In the seeking process, it is vital to continually refine our sources.

#ThriveOnline

out information from specific sources. We can subscribe to newsletters from professional associations in our discipline or use some type of real simple syndication (RSS) reader to receive all relevant "feeds" from various sources within a single service. Second, we can use social media (e.g., Twitter) to follow organizations and individuals we consider credible and tap into the power of the "stream" on an on-demand basis. We would not ever expect to keep up with everything that is happening on Twitter, but we can follow credible individuals who have the potential to provide valuable information each time we visit.

In the seeking process, it is vital to continually refine our sources. Just about every news service has played wolf with its claims that a story is "breaking" news. As we become interested in a new topic, we will need to build a foundation of subject matter networks within the new domain.

When I am in the middle of an intense academic research project, I often subscribe to the RSS feeds from relevant journals. The publishers rarely send the full articles, because they are most often behind paywalls. However, I can quickly browse the titles to see if there are any articles that I should read using our library's database access.

Sense

The next part of the PKM process involves making sense of the information that has been gathered in the seek phase. When we make sense of information, it becomes personal to us. We reflect on it and compare and contrast it to what we have come to know from prior learning through PKM.

As we are making sense of the information, we determine whether to store it for future reference. Those data points that are considered potentially important to our future needs are categorized into new or existing taxonomies in either a public or private way. Social bookmarking services allow us to save articles, videos, and other information stored across the Internet and bookmark the information for future use. Tags can also be applied, which makes locating the information more manageable in the future.

When conducting formal academic research, I prefer to use a references manager. I like Zotero, but many other options exist for research-oriented writing. The primary reason I place items involved in this kind of work within Zotero is that it reduces the time required to cite sources in a given citation style. Also, Zotero can auto-generate a list of references of each source that was cited in a paper. This list automatically updates as revisions are made and new citations are included.

Sensing also involves experimentation. When we come across something new in our seeking, our sensing gives us time to try out the new thing and see where it may fit with our existing practices or knowledge. We can try these experiments on our own or invite others to work as a team in this more creative part of the process.

Share

The final stage of PKM is share. Jarche (2014) describes that after we seek and sense

we later share our creations, first with our teams and perhaps later with our communities of practice or even our networks. We use our understanding of our communities and networks to discern with whom and when to share our knowledge. It's like constantly breathing in and out. (para. 16)

We may determine that our students would benefit from an article that we have discovered, but we may find that we need to explain caveats to some of its assertions. A video we have created that explains a particularly challenging concept in our online course may be valuable to those who are in a more advanced course than the one we are teaching, so we decide to make it publicly available, even outside the LMS.

The sharing process also helps us build more community and connect with those who have common research interests, such as a passion for teaching. Especially when teaching online, we can feel disconnected from our cohort of others engaged in the work that we do. We may not have opportunities for informal conversation in the hallway at our institution, but we can use PKM to build a network of people who can contribute to our ongoing learning.

Opportunity to Connect

Search for #ThriveOnline. See if there are individuals you might like to follow on Twitter who share interests similar to yours or might provide you with a unique perspective on an issue.

And So It Goes

Once a PKM has been established, we continually go through the process of seeking, sensing, and sharing without ever reaching a finish line. We seek our information from a PLN and other valued sources. We make sense of that information and transform it into knowledge by questioning it, comparing and contrasting it to other sources we have gathered in the past, and experimenting with it by doing and creating. Finally, we share to others we work closely with, to our students, and even in public ways through social and other media.

Jarche (2014) stresses the habits of PKM and what happens if only individual pieces of the framework are used:

> If you only seek information, you are just a consumer. If you seek and share, then you are a re-broadcaster, adding little value. If you seek and make sense of information, without sharing, you are missing out on opportunities to learn and connect. While we cannot seek, sense, share in all aspects of our lives, there are some areas where it is important to do so. (para. 18)

PKM helps us be more productive by aligning our focus on seeking sources that will be more relevant and credible in our work, making sense of that information and translating it into knowledge, and sharing what we have learned with others. See Box 3.1 for an example.

Box 3.1
A PKM Example

In describing PKM, it can sometimes be difficult to see what it really looks like in practice. Here's an example of how a professor could use PKM to get ready to teach a new course. In this example, when Bjorn taught consumer behavior for the first time, he used all three parts of PKM.

Seek

The first seeking Bjorn did involved taking advice from Therese Huston (2012), the author of *Teaching What You Don't Know*. She suggests that the first time we teach a class, we seek out syllabi from five other professors who have taught the course before. These syllabi each contain their own curated prescriptions for resources to explore. Bjorn gathered some syllabi and found several relevant videos that he had not been previously aware of. The assignments that were given to students gave him a broader perspective on how he might assess his students' learning.

He also subscribed on an RSS reader to feeds dealing with consumer behavior. The textbook he adopted offered an RSS feed as well, which released multiple articles each week throughout the semester. In addition, he already had subscribed to marketing feeds that often related to consumer behavior.

Doug McKee shared on his Teach Better blog his experience teaching an econometrics course and how he has his students participate in a poster session event. As Bjorn read Doug's blog, he instantly started thinking about how this approach might apply to some aspect of his teaching.

(*Continues*)

Box 3.1 (*Continued*)

Sense

When Bjorn found an article that he thought might serve as an excellent resource for his class, he saved it to his social bookmarking tool. He used the name/number of the class as one tag that he applied to each article (MRKT369). He also included a tag for video because sometimes he wanted to pull up all the videos that he had saved that relate to a particular course.

Bjorn studied the tables of contents from the multiple textbooks that he was reviewing for his course. As he sought out new information and began to make sense of it, his own framework for how he might sequence the course started to take shape.

Bjorn bookmarked all of Doug McKee's posts about the poster session event. They corresponded a bit over Twitter, and Doug suggested that Bjorn might struggle with trying to conduct a poster session event without having the digital displays Doug was able to use at his institution. Bjorn reflected on how he could take the best aspects of what he was able to create in his class's experience while still adapting it for a smaller and less-resourced community.

Share

Most of Bjorn's sharing took place through the teaching of the course. He was able to incorporate timely examples throughout the semester because he had categorized the information and made it easy to retrieve when we entered a new part of the course. As students discovered their own examples of resources that were relevant to the course, he could pass those examples on to other students, or save them as inspiration for future classes.

CONSISTENTLY SEEK, SENSE, AND SHARE RELEVANT INFORMATION IN YOUR CLASSES

When we have well-established PKM, our online courses can be that much more vibrant with current, relevant examples. We can also continually improve our pedagogical effectiveness by seeking out information about the scholarship of teaching and learning and then sharing our successes and failures. Finally, we can experience more richness in our lives, as we pursue learning that is most closely aligned with our passions and interests.

Seek

When we reflect on the process of seeking, many of us think of it as an action we take immediately when we have a question about a topic. For example, we may have a question from a student we do not know the answer to. We then head over to our trusted Google search engine to research the answer.

The problem with relying solely on web searches as a method of seeking is that we are not always aware which questions to ask within a given domain. What do you search for when you are not even really sure of your question? How do you unravel the mysteries of a topic that does not have well-established, agreed-on answers, or even questions?

The Stream
Broadly speaking, there are two methods of seeking that can be employed. First, you can leverage established

connections and "dip your toe" in a stream of information. In this case, you will not be able to keep up with all
the data flowing across that stream of information. However, you can build a trusted network, often referred to as
a PLN, and have access to community-based knowledge at
any time.

Twitter uses the analogy of a stream when describing the collected information that is posted by its users.
Each time users compose and publish a tweet, it gets
added to their individual streams. It is recommended that
we tweet multiple times a day because the likelihood of
someone seeing an individual tweet is relatively small.
There are also tools that help us automate this process
of tweeting multiple times a day, making it that much
more challenging to ever think we could "keep up" with
Twitter.

The mind-set of attempting to read everything is
not helpful. However, we can create lists on Twitter that
allow us to categorize our network connections in a more
granular way. Peter Newbury (n.d.) has a Twitter list of
teaching and learning centers that can be helpful if we
want our focus to be grounded in evidence-based teaching methods, for example. You can make your own list or
subscribe to others that are most relevant to your learning
pursuits.

RSS

The second method of seeking is made possible through
a technology called RSS. Using RSS, we can subscribe to
websites with information that we do not want to miss.
Many of us used to subscribe to newspapers. I remember
valuing the business section, but not getting much from

the sports section. With RSS, I get to specify precisely the kind of information I find important and have it all come into one place using an RSS reader app.

RSS lets us skim over the headlines of everything that happened within our network since the last time we checked in. We likely will not ever read every story that gets published into a news reader, but we are able to capture those gems that may very well have been missed if we were relying solely on checking into a social media stream.

Almost every website that we might visit today has RSS already built into it. This includes popular news sites such as the *New York Times*, the *Economist*, and the BBC. It also includes our cousin's blog about his trip to Alaska, along with every picture he took on the trip.

Instead of having to visit a website to see if it has recently published new stories that speak to our interest we can subscribe to that website's RSS feed and have relevant information available for us. We can consolidate all the information we want to be kept up to date on in a single place, called a news aggregator or feed reader.

Academic journals often have RSS feeds built into their websites as well. I do not regularly subscribe to these feeds unless I am in the midst of conducting related research. One of the things we can do to ensure a healthy PKM system is to continually refine it to meet our needs most effectively. See thriveonlineseries.com for recommended tools for subscribing to and reading RSS feeds.

RSS Reader

Popular news aggregators (RSS readers), such as Feedly, keep track of which stories we have already read and which ones are unread and should be called more to our attention. RSS feeds are stored within Feedly. Each time a new story is published it is pushed into Feedly and is waiting for us the next time we open the Feedly app or view the Feedly website on our browser. It is not necessary to visit every blog, news site, or other online resource to see if they have recently added a new post. All the new content gets compiled into the RSS reader, giving you a single place to check.

Once you have subscribed to some of your favorite news sources on Feedly, you might find it helpful to begin to categorize them. You might have categories for general teaching articles, ones related to the higher education industry, and even specific folders related to each of your courses.

Podcast Catcher

Another excellent source of learning involves podcasts. Instead of needing to have our eyes fixed on the written word, we can fill our ears with audio content. Listening to podcasts is very similar to listening to the radio. However, you no longer have to tune in according to the radio station's schedule. You can listen on demand.

My podcast is called *Teaching in Higher Ed* (teachinginhighered.com). It has aired weekly since June 2014. People have told me that they appreciate the ability to learn more about how to effectively facilitate learning by listening to the podcast. They especially enjoy how they can take this knowledge in while they are driving in their cars, washing dishes, going for a walk, or waiting for their kid's soccer game to finish.

Podcasts can be subscribed to on RSS readers, but that is not the most ideal way to experience them. Instead, use what is known as a podcast catcher app. These applications capture all of the latest episodes of your favorite podcasts and collect them in one place. Podcast catcher apps are already installed on most smartphones, so that the audio content can be transported along with the listener in a car, on public transportation, or on a walk around the neighborhood. As each episode is listened to, it is removed from the device, which frees up space for other podcasts to be stored. There is the capability to save episodes for future reference. Setting up playlists will enable the podcasts to be played in order of preference.

If you are an iPhone user, you more than likely already have a podcast app on your phone, perhaps without even realizing it. If the podcast app was removed at some point, you can easily search for it on the App Store and reinstall it on your phone. Once you locate the app, you will be well on your way to a whole new way of accessing learning. As you get more experienced listening to podcasts, you may want to try out other podcast catchers. Overcast works similarly to the built-in podcast, with the added benefit of its smart speed feature, which removes superfluous pauses and lets you speed up the playback of podcast recordings without making people sound like The Chipmunks.

I keep an updated list of my favorite podcasts on the *Teaching in Higher Ed* website at teachinginhighered.com/podcastgreats.

Invitation to Connect

What are some of your favorite higher education podcasts? Share these using #ThriveOnline.

Social Media

Sites such as Twitter and Facebook can bring out the best and worst that humanity has to offer. The value we receive is often in direct proportion to the people and organizations we decide to follow. While news organizations have entire teams devoted to their social media presence, individuals who curate stories often have unique perspectives to share.

Twitter

Twitter is a social network created with the idea of using text to communicate with multiple people at once. The founders were intrigued by the idea of knowing the status of their friends at any given time. As they were coming up with a name, Twitter resonated because it means "a short burst of inconsequential information" and "chirps from birds" (Dearnell, 2019 , para. 1). When birds chirp to each other, the noises do not express meaning to the untrained ear. However, to the bird receiving the tweet, the message is significant.

The first step in getting started on Twitter is to set up an account and create a profile. Real names are not required, and some academics have had fun expressing alter egos on the service (e.g., Shit Academics Say: @AcademicsSay). The @ symbol precedes a person's username. People can tag other users in a tweet to call attention to it by including the person's @username in their message. When users don't have some type of profile picture (even if it isn't of a person) it raises suspicions that the account is not authentic, so get a photo or graphic uploaded as you are setting up your account.

It is possible to set up a Twitter account to have all of the tweets that are sent maintained as private on the service. Although this can be a legitimate choice, especially given the cyberbullying and harassment that can occur, this setting does somewhat negate the value of networked learning that Twitter affords.

After setting up a profile, it is time to start following people and organizations. Keeping the list of who gets followed to around 10 to 20 to begin with will help you get familiarized with the service without becoming too overwhelmed. In addition to following users, you can use hashtags to observe and participate in conversations around particular subjects. A hashtag is preceded by the symbol #, such as #Highered, #EdTech, or #ProdChat (a chat for those interested in productivity).

Productive online professors keep limits on how long we spend on social media. The value in using it may be achieved only if we do not let it get in the way of other ways to spend our time.

Facebook

Sixty-eight percent of the U.S. population uses Facebook (Pew Research Center, 2017). While the social network is

Productive online professors keep limits on how long we spend on social media.

#ThriveOnline

primarily thought of as for use on a personal basis, it does make sense to align one's interests and professional goals with pages followed. Unlike Twitter, Facebook requires members to use their real name in their profile. There are people who have gotten around these restrictions, but there is always the possibility of getting locked out of Facebook for not adhering to the rules. Set up an account using your real name and concentrate on adjusting the privacy settings to your liking.

I do not find Facebook as essential in my PKM system as I do Twitter. The fact that I find less value in it means that I am at my most productive when I limit the time I spend on this social network. We can experience the "fear of missing out" (often abbreviated as FOMO in Internet humor) when it comes to social media. It helps to remember that these companies' business models are predicated on capitalizing on our desire to stay caught up on everything.

Sense

It can be tempting to stop after the seek process, thinking we are done. If what we are desiring is a deeper form of learning, we must continue to the process of sense-making. Part of making sense of the information we have gleaned is to store it within the system that will make it easy for us to locate in the future, as well as view it in the context of other knowledge we have acquired on the same subject.

There is an option in most modern web browsers to save bookmarks for links to be able to refer to later. In some cases, those bookmarks can even travel from your computer's web browser right over to the browser on your smartphone. However, that is where most of the feature sets end related to saving links/bookmarks, and we can be left wanting.

Social Bookmarking

One of the greatest advantages of social bookmarking tools is the ability to future-proof them in multiple ways. Tags may be used to categorize articles. This is akin to placing them in a manila folder like many of us used to do to save a magazine article for future use. However, an article can have multiple tags assigned to it, so that it can be searched for numerous ways. You can tag articles by class number (e.g., BUSN114, MRKT369, or MGMT470) and by the type of item being saved (e.g., video, audio, or blog).

One downside to bookmarking articles of interest is that the site may delete the information in the future, or the link that houses the data may change. Clicking a link to an article that no longer exists on a web page will result in what is called a 404 error. That message indicates that the link that is being accessed is no longer stored in the same place as it was previously, or that it has been deleted entirely.

This downside may be negated by using a notebook application to store entire articles, not just the link to articles. Bookmarking services that have the capability of archiving articles directly on their service can also be a helpful way of avoiding 404 errors and disappearing items stored on the Internet. One extreme example of this challenge is when a website changes its entire structure for storing information on its site. What used to be site.com/folder/date/link might update to site.com/date/ link, and any bookmarks that were saved under the prior organizational scheme are now lost.

While there are tremendous benefits to having information that you have found valuable enough to save in an easy-to-search repository, the power of having a robust set of bookmarks can grow exponentially when you get connected with others in your PLN and can share bookmarks together.

THREE STEPS TO SOCIAL BOOKMARKING

It is easy to get started with social bookmarking. First, create an account on whatever service you have chosen. Second, install the bookmarking service's extension within your preferred web browser. An extension is a mini program that runs alongside your browser and performs specific functions. A bookmarking extension installs a button within your browser, and each time you click on it, it will bring up a dialog box that allows you to save the link on your bookmarking service without ever having to leave the page being viewed. After the extension is installed on your browser, you are ready to pursue step three and to start saving bookmarks and tags all in one place.

Pinboard.in

Pinboard.in is a social bookmarking service that takes the spotlight for its simplicity and scalability. It can easily bookmark sites, using its browser extension, and share extensions on smartphones. Bookmarks may be saved as public (viewable to others) or private (visible only to you).

An ever-growing tag cloud is displayed on the right side of the Pinboard site. Tags can be clicked on, making it easy to navigate directly to a tag of interest. There is also a search feature, which allows searching by tag or throughout your bookmarked content.

A paid Pinboard account includes a feature that overcomes the downside of saving a simple bookmark directly in a browser. If links that have been collected on Pinboard change in the future, the content that was stored on the page is still accessible from within Pinboard. Each time a web page is saved, the materials from the page are saved on Pinboard and archived, should the original page's location change or be deleted.

Diigo

Diigo is a terrific bookmarking service for people who always like to keep a highlighter nearby. Instead of marking up a paper copy of an article of interest, Diigo can be used to highlight directly on top of a web page or to make other notes. Highlights and annotations are saved for future reference and can be shared with others.

When saving a web page to Diigo, tags may be added directly from a web browser (after installing the extension). Diigo also has an outliner tool that helps organize bookmarks and other information when researching a topic with organization needs that extend beyond tags. Diigo also has capabilities for annotating PDFs and screenshots of web pages, directly within a web browser. Having highlighted and annotated articles on our smartphones and tablets ensures that wherever we take these devices we will always have the information when it is needed.

Notebook Application

When you do not want to share information publicly, at least not from its original source, a notebook application can be a valuable tool. Just like physical notebooks that store hard copies of information, notebook applications can be used to store virtual copies of data.

Regardless of the operating system, your computer probably came with a simple notes application already installed (e.g., Notepad on Windows and Notes on Mac). However, the features on these free applications may not be sufficient for managing information in a robust PKM system. The following are features that should be included on whatever notebook application you choose:

- *Cloud-based*: The notebook application should be available on your computer of choice, your smart-phone, and a browser.
- *Quick capture*: It should be easy to capture different kinds of information, including pictures, web content, audio, and even handwritten sketches.
- *Integration*: All of your commonly used apps should have the ability to integrate with your chosen notebook application.

If you already subscribe to Microsoft's Office 365, which includes OneNote, or have access to a copy of OneNote, you can use this terrific option for a notes application. It has a lot of similarities to the physical note-books many of us used to set up for our classes in school, such as adding notebooks and pages to keep your information organized.

Another popular notebook system is called Evernote. It offers a plethora of capturing options, including taking photos, adding photos from your library, recording audio, attaching files, and even capturing notes that you have written on sticky notes and categorizing those notes in a way that you specify. It will also take a picture of a document that is resting on a contrasting background and automatically straighten it, crop the image to contain only the document, and increase the crispness of the text.

See thriveonlineseries.com for a list of recommended social bookmarking and note-taking applications.

Invitation to Connect

What do you use for your digital note-taking system, or what are you planning on experimenting with after seeing the recommendations on thriveonlineseries.com? Share using #ThriveOnline.

Share

After finding information and transforming it into knowledge through sensing, it is time to share what we have learned. It can be challenging to take the risks involved to share our discoveries. Imposter syndrome can set in. We may not perceive what we have to offer as being valuable. The fear of looking foolish or making mistakes may hold us back from diving in.

Nothing is wrong with being a lurker when you are first exposed to a new environment. Block (2017) recommends holding back from sharing ideas when we are new in a role, lest we seem disrespectful to those who have a better context of what has worked in the past and where some of the political land mines can be.

However, after being in an observer role for a while, the most significant learning and growth can be achieved by taking the risk to share in various ways. One practice that aligns well with sharing is what is known as "working out loud." When we work out loud, we share our successes and failures in an iterative way and in public spaces. My *Teaching and Higher Ed* podcast and blog are the primary way that I work out loud and incorporate the sensing and sharing part of PKM. Stepper (2014) states that the origins of the phrase *working out loud* came from the idea of sharing one's work online. He eventually refined his definition to more broadly include the importance of relationships and engagement. Stepper (2016) describes the practice as follows:

> Working out loud is an approach to building relationships that help you in some way. It's a practice that combines conventional wisdom about relationships with modern ways to reach and engage people. When you work out loud, you feel good and empowered at the same time. (para. 10)

When working out loud, we still take in information, but we also ask what value we can provide to others while still extending our own learning. We make our work visible to a network of people with interests and passions similar to our own. Stepper (2014) emphasizes

> making your work visible in such a way that it might help others. When you do that—when you work in a more open, connected way—you can build a purposeful network that makes you more effective and provides access to more opportunities. (para. 13)

It is risky and takes dedication to work out loud, but the benefits are abundant.

Some educators have modified the phrase to better reflect our specific work. "Teaching out loud" is when we share our teaching experiences with our PLNs and others in such a way as to improve the profession overall. Doug McKee, who teaches economics at Cornell University, regularly blogs about his classes after receiving the student course evaluations. These are some examples of feedback he has shared on his blog:

> [McKee was] rambling and nervous in class. Unclear and rushed when teaching math.
>
> Pretty atrocious class. Take it if you must.
>
> He really cares a lot about teaching but still needs to find a more effective way of doing it.
>
> Prof. McKee likes to think he is a conscious, self-aware teacher. And he's really a nice guy, smiles, and talks at a very slow pace. Yet for some reason, he is not great at explaining

difficult concepts he expects students to solve in exams—he rushes through the explanations.

The kind of courage McKee (2015) showed in sharing this feedback, publicly, on his blog is marvelous. He went on to describe how he extracts value from course evaluations in a systematic way. He concluded with some qualitative input he hangs on to in order to remember that he was able to reach some students:

> The role of a teacher isn't to deliver information, but to excite their students to want to learn, make every student feel accountable for his/her learning, guide the social process of learning. And you nailed that. Thanks professor. (para. 19)

McKee reflects on his own practice as he employs teaching out loud, yet he also pushes his readers to do soul-searching of their own and to continue to refine their own approaches. McKee (2016) stresses, "Teaching is a creative process, and if you're not creating, you're doing it wrong" (para. 6). He also shares his experiences at various teaching conferences, passing along what he gains from having attended. What a tremendous example of how sharing benefits the giver and all the receivers.

TAKE ACTION: FINDING, CURATING, AND SHARING KNOWLEDGE

This is an opportunity to reflect on which steps are most important to take after reading through Part Three. Here are specific next actions you may want to record either in your task manager or in a someday/maybe list to increase the impact of having read this book:

❑ Explore Harold Jarche's PKM resources on his website, including the videos he has with further information. The link may be found on the book website at thriveonlineseries.com.

❑ Set up a PKM process, and identify tools to help you seek, sense, and share your knowledge.

❑ Create an account on Feedly (or another popular RSS reader) and subscribe to blogs you want to be consolidated into a single place. Most academic journals have RSS feeds, too. Thus, when reading your custom newspaper on Feedly, you will be alerted that the latest issue of a favorite journal has been released and what articles are included. If the journal has a paywall, you will not be able to read the articles on Feedly, but you can be reminded to take a look within whatever service you usually use to read academic journals.

❑ Assess your use of social media and whether or not it makes sense to use a new service to cultivate a more robust PLN.

❑ Use a social bookmarking tool, such as Pinboard.in or Diigo, and start saving articles with tags for a better means to locate them in the future.

❑ Curate what you are discovering through your PKM process and share the learning by writing a blog post.

❑ Start using a podcast catcher app (e.g., Apple Podcasts, Google Play, Stitcher, or Pocket Casts) and subscribe to a few higher education podcasts (e.g., my podcast, *Teaching in Higher Ed*).

❑ Share some of your favorite higher education podcasts using #ThriveOnline.

❑ Visit the Thrive Online website at thriveonlineseries .com to discover other PKM tools you may want to explore.

PART FOUR

LEVERAGING TECHNOLOGY TOWARD GREATER PRODUCTIVITY

LEVERAGING TECHNOLOGY TOWARD GREATER PRODUCTIVITY

We have looked at various types of technology to support getting more of our priorities accomplished, productively pursuing lifelong learning through PKM, and ways to use technology toward improved communication in our classes. Now we look toward other ways to use technology to reduce some of the friction in our work.

The methods for pursuing productivity presented in this part are more about the seemingly little steps we can take that add up to big results. As Amy Cavender (2013), who writes for *The Chronicle of Higher Education's* productivity blog ProfHacker, points out,

Some of the challenges we face in our daily work are major, requiring considerable effort to resolve—and we feel a justifiable sense of accomplishment when we meet those challenges successfully.

Sometimes, though, there's something very small that might help us or someone else do something a little better. (para. 1–2)

What tools and techniques are available to increase our efficiency in online instruction without losing the desired effectiveness? Part Four addresses approaches such as batch processing, checklists, and workflows as levers for getting more done. It also considers ways to approach grading that foster the connections we desire with our students while keeping us as productive as possible in the process.

BATCH PROCESSING

One practice that can slow us down in our work is shifting from one task to the next without regard to the way in which we might group our tasks for greater efficiency. If I am going to log into our LMS, it makes sense for me to take care of all the small actions I need to while I am in there. If I am going to check email, I can do that most efficiently by blocking off times during the day to focus on that task and then closing the application down so that I am not distracted by every subsequent email that arrives.

The principle behind batch processing is that if we are going to work with a series of tools, it makes sense to perform all the tasks that involve those applications during the same work session.

#ThriveOnline

The principle behind batch processing is that if we are going to work with a series of tools, it makes sense to perform all the tasks that involve those applications during the same work session. Some people cook in batches to make meal preparation more efficient. The phrase *batch processing* is also used in the technological realm when a series of computing tasks are run together without a human needing to intervene. Thinking through related tasks and performing them at the same time can greatly boost productivity.

As Kathryn E. Linder (2017) emphasizes on her *You've Got This* podcast,

> When I am working with a strategy, I think about, "What is something that I can do a massive amount of at one time and it is going to be better for me in the long run?" . . . [The] first strategy of batching is answering the question, "What's best done in bulk?" [So] what are the things in your life that could be done in bulk? (1:08)

To cite an absurd example, but one that brings the point home, while you are at the grocery store (a location-based context), it makes sense to pick up all the items you need, rather than having to go back and forth between your home and the store until you remember and pick up everything you need.

Contexts

A small way to leverage batch processing is to identify contexts within your task management system. Most task management systems have a field that can be used to indicate what tools would be needed to complete a particular action. We need access to the Internet and our LMS to grade students' assignments that were submitted online. A phone is necessary to return a call. Sometimes, it is not a tool, but rather a place where you would need to be to perform a given task. We need to be at the pharmacy to pick up the medication we have been prescribed. I can return a library book only if I am at the library (unless I have delegated that task to someone else).

Context is often symbolized by an @ symbol within task management systems. You might use @agendas to keep track of what topics need to be discussed at upcoming meetings you are responsible for facilitating. You might use @errands to keep track of what errands you need to run. When you need to follow up with people about an item, they can be listed as a context (@Dave, @Julio, @Julia). When you delegate an item to a person, you can list that as Waiting: Dave, for example, to be able to identify delegated items when speaking with individuals or in following up with them.

David Allen (2015) describes four criteria to use when choosing what action to work on next:

1. *Context*: What tools do you need to perform the task (@phone, @online, @email)?
2. *Time*: How much time do you have to work on a given task (15 minutes, 1 hour, 2 hours)?
3. *Energy*: What kind of attention/focus do you have to devote to a task (task requires concentration, like writing, or more mindless, like folding laundry)?

4. *Priority*: If, after considering context, time, and energy, you are left with a decision point, which task is most important (high, medium, low)?

A couple of other ways of grouping contexts to make batch processing easier are discussed next.

Location-Based Contexts

For tasks that you can do only at home, @home can be set up, while @work may be used for actions that may be taken only while you are at work. The nice part about using location-based contexts is that many task management services offer smartphone applications that are designed to take advantage of your phone's location-awareness features.

As you arrive at work, you can have your phone give you a little nudge to remind you of those tasks that can be performed only while you are there. Alternatively, you can have your phone tell you to preheat the oven or any number of other tasks when you get home.

Application-Based Contexts

Another way to apply batch processing is to consider what needs to get done within a given application or service. One example that comes up most often for me is regarding our LMS. Once I have already logged in to the LMS, it makes sense to take care of other items that can be completed only while working in the LMS.

When I am designing a new course, I often use a video-creation tool, a slide deck application, a word processor, and our LMS. By having those applications open as I am working, I can minimize the time it takes to move from one part of the design process to the next.

If an email needs to be sent to someone, it makes sense to wait until you have a few more you need to send or until the next scheduled time you have to check email. Otherwise, the act of checking email is bound to present you with distractions galore, as discussed in Part Two.

CHECKLISTS

Another terrific method for boosting our productivity and reducing friction in our work is the simple act of constructing checklists for steps we take on a regular basis. A checklist can be used for something as simple as packing for a trip as well as for more complicated tasks, such as ensuring the necessary steps have been taken during surgery to keep a patient safe. It can seem counterintuitive to use a checklist in online teaching. If we need a list to tell us what to do, especially if we have taught a given class multiple times, it may raise the question of whether we are doing a good job. However, there is much to be gained from studying how checklists are having a tremendous impact in fields such as medicine. In the following sections, we discuss those benefits as well as how checklists can benefit our teaching.

Checklists Save Lives—Really!

In 2008, Atul Gawande began researching the effects of using a 2-minute checklist with teams of people involved in performing surgeries. The results were significant. The number of deaths was reduced by 47% in the 8 hospitals involved in the study.

When first hearing about Gawande's (2010) *New York Times*–best-selling book on checklists, *The Checklist Manifesto*, it seemed implausible to me that there could be such an increase in lives saved all because of something as simple as double-checking a series of simple steps. Gawande, a surgeon, was first intrigued by checklists after learning about a doctor who had saved the life of a child who had fallen into a frozen pond. The physician's lifesaving efforts were all constructed around a checklist, and Gawande wanted to know more.

Gawande admitted to his reluctance to use a checklist before, during, and after his surgeries, given his decades of experience. He shared on NPR's Morning Edition his surprise at the results he achieved through the use of the World Health Organization's Surgical Safety Checklist: "I didn't expect it," Gawande said with a chuckle.

> It's massively improved the kind of results that I'm getting. When we implemented this checklist in eight other hospitals, I started using it because I didn't want to be a hypocrite. But hey, I'm at Harvard, did I need a checklist? No. (Inskeep & Brand, 2010, para. 28)

Or so he thought. After using a presurgery checklist he now sees the results of the choice. Gawande shared the radical impact of the checklist, revealing "I have not gotten through a week of surgery where the checklist has not caught a problem" (Inskeep & Brand, 2010, para. 30).

A Checklist for Checklists

Gawande (2010) illustrates the characteristics of effective checklists:

> Good checklists . . . are precise. They are efficient, to the point, and easy to use even in the most difficult situations. They do not try to spell out everything—a checklist cannot fly a plane. Instead, they provide reminders of only the most critical and important steps—the ones that even the highly skilled professional using them could miss. Good checklists are, above all, practical. (p. 120)

Gawande collaborated with Dan Boorman of Boeing to come up with a checklist for checklists. They recommend three domains of checklist creation: development, drafting, and validation.

In the development phase, they prescribe that a checklist have clear, concise objectives, as well as stress the importance of including items that will facilitate more effective communication among those involved. The drafting suggestions include the need for a readable font and the use of so-called pause points (breaks in the workflow). If we have more than 7 to 10 items in a checklist before pausing to check in on our progress, we tend to stop paying attention to where we are in the flow (thereby negating some of the benefits of using a checklist). Validation involves steps that can be taken to ensure that the checklist is useful, such as having a plan for revisions and ensuring that the checklist can be completed within an appropriate time frame.

Checklists for Professors

It is not even necessary to read about all of the lives that have been saved through medical and other checklists to get on board with the idea of using checklists in our teaching. Many of us have been using various kinds of checklists for years, but Gawande's (2010) *The Checklist Manifesto* provides guidance on how to think more carefully about constructing them.

A sample collection of types of checklists that may be used in higher education teaching, as well as some of the items included on each checklist, is found in Box 4.1.

Box 4.1 Sample Checklists for Various Contexts

❑ **Prep: Academic Year**—Revise curriculum vitae (CV); review conference possibilities; review institution's website for needed revisions.

❑ **Prep: Semester**—Select textbooks; create a weekly schedule; update website items.

❑ **Prep: Class**—Review course learning objectives; create/revise syllabus; write/revise exams; request publisher materials; send welcome message.

❑ **Publish: Podcast Episode**—Determine and record episode's recommendation; enter episode number in calendar; send confirmation email to guest; send thank-you to podcast guest.

❑ **Set-up: New Teaching Assistant (TA)**—Introduce TA to students in the course; share TA Dropbox folder with TA; add TA to all courses in LMS.

❑ **Follow-up: Conference**—Write blog post about conference; complete expense report and other forms; send items to office for reimbursement.

More sample checklists are included on thriveonlineseries .com, along with other resources that will assist in creating new checklists. *The Chronicle of Higher Education*'s Prof-Hacker blog also includes resources for those interested in checklists relevant to those of us in higher education. Watrall (2009) shares his end-of-semester checklist, which consists of the following steps:

1. Backup my course websites
2. Update my CV
3. Write an "End of Semester Roundup" post on [my] blog
4. Shred exams/papers from X number of semesters ago
5. Backup my class materials

Houston (2011) also shares about the use of checklists on the ProfHacker blog. She describes the following types of checklists:

- **Read-Do:** Read each step of the task, and then perform them in order, checking them off as you go, like following a recipe.
- **Do-Confirm:** Perform steps of the task from memory until you reach a defined pause point, when you go through the checklist and confirm that each step has been completed. (para. 6)

My teaching-related checklists tend to be more oriented toward read-do types, while my podcast episode checklist is more helpful as a do-confirm list, where I take the opportunity to make sure I haven't forgotten any step that is needed to successfully publish a new episode of the *Teaching in Higher Ed* podcast.

WORKFLOWS

A workflow is the name for when a series of steps are thought through and made more efficient. Technology is often used in creating workflows to allow the series of steps to be completed without us needing to give the step-by-step instructions or commands. Workflow apps are services that address wasted time by repeating steps. Leveraging these types of tools can be as simple as automating the process of receiving a text message in the morning to remind us to bring an umbrella on days when it rains or as sophisticated as processing requests for letters of recommendation. The following sections provide an overview of how to use forms to streamline processes, how to automate common tasks, and how to build a more sophisticated workflow.

Build a Form

You do not have to be highly technically proficient to take advantage of the power of workflows. Forms provide an easy way to gather data and shorten the length of time it takes to receive the type of input being sought.

I have a form that I ask students to fill out when they are requesting a reference for applying to an academic program or are asking me for a letter of recommendation. It includes all the information that I will need to respond efficiently and accurately to their request, which has dramatically reduced the back-and-forth emails I used to encounter before implementing the form. See the book series website at thriveonlineseries.com for my reference form.

Another way to build a workflow is to automate some portion of your work.

#ThriveOnline

Automate

Another way to build a workflow is to automate some portion of your work. You might create an automated means for saving an essential email as a PDF for archival purposes or use an online automation service.

IFTTT

The service If This Then That (IFTT; ifttt.com) is an online automation service. What tasks might benefit from automation are limited only by our imagination. We can construct a command that says, "If this thing happens over here, then make that thing happen over there." Think of IFTTT as a connector between multiple services and devices. It helps them interact with each other and cause things to happen. Examples of automated actions available through what IFTTT calls "applets" (little applications) are as follows:

- Log a completed Uber trip on a spreadsheet.
- Get a text with the weather report each morning.
- Get a text when it is going to rain the next day.
- Save all new Instagram photos you post on Google photos.
- Automatically save tweets that you mark as a favorite on a social bookmarking service.

Cavender (2016b) reports that she uses IFTTT to automatically cross-post her ProfHacker blog posts onto her personal site. That way, she can have more current content on her website than she otherwise might. Her IFTTT applet (workflow) watches to see whenever a new Prof-Hacker post comes out with her byline. Then, it takes that same post and adds it to her personal website. She appends each of the blog titles to state "My Latest at Prof-Hacker," so readers are aware that the content has also been posted elsewhere.

I set up IFTTT to automatically add any tweet that I favorite on Twitter into my preferred social bookmarking service (Pinboard.in). If the tweet includes a hashtag (e.g., #HigherEd), the category automatically gets included on that bookmark within Pinboard. Weekly I add additional tags on Pinboard to bookmarks that have recently been added to make it that much easier to find information in the future. This collection of continually updated bookmarks helps me in class planning as I look to bring rich content into my online courses.

Zapier

Another web automation app is Zapier. This tool integrates with hundreds of apps and services and allows for a series of steps on other services to take place. Instead of needing to be a programmer to automate tasks on the web, Zapier may be used to "connect your apps, so they can work together" (Zapier, n.d., para. 1). ProfHacker author Anastasia Salter (2014) uses Zapier to connect Twitter with her bookmarking service. When new tweets are sent out on some of her favorite hashtags, she uses Zapier to categorize and save them for easier archiving and analysis.

I do not use IFTTT or Zapier much in managing student work because my LMS (Canvas) does such an effective job of that for me. It has a tool called Speed Grader that is integrated into the LMS that lives up to its name. Instead, I prefer to use IFTTT and Zapier to reduce friction in other parts of my life.

Invitation to Connect

Have you made use of any automated services like IFTTT or Zapier to accomplish tasks in your work? What has been your experience using them? Share your thoughts using #ThriveOnline.

TEXT EXPANSION APPLICATIONS

Another way of using technology to be more productive is through a text expansion application. Most computers and smartphones have a kind of text expansion built in, though it is much simpler than the more full-featured applications. For example, the iPhone has autocorrect to fix simple typing mistakes. If I type *teh* when I mean *the*, the program corrects it for me.

However, a dedicated text expansion application can provide even greater time-saving features than the built-in ones on many phones and computers. Peacock (2015) explains the benefits of using a text expansion application as follows:

> Do you find yourself typing the exact same phrase multiple times each day or sending [a nearly] iden-
> tical email to various people? Do you make the same strange spelling mistake over and over? Do you get annoyed hunting for special characters for a word or phrase you type often?

Then text expansion may be the solution for you. (para. 1–2)

When we find ourselves repeatedly typing the same text, we can come up with a snippet, a small bit of text, to type every time we want to have that text pasted in whatever application we are working in. Pham (2014) writes, "You can think of it as a more sophisticated version of 'auto-correct' that you can customize to your particular needs" (para. 4). Text expansion applications automate the entering of text. It could be just a few characters used as an abbreviation, or some other short set of letters (e.g., when I type *b@vu*, the app automatically changes that text into my work email address). Text expansion apps can enter even more text than that, saving us even more time. When I type *tiheslack* in an email, for example, the app automatically turns that into the following introduction to our Teaching in Higher Ed Slack community:

Dear [name],

Thanks for your interest in being a part of the Teaching in Higher Ed community on Slack. I've added you to our channel and look forward to connecting with you there.

When you first accept the invite, you will be automatically added to the two, default channels: #general and #random. I highly suggest looking on the left-hand side of the Slack application window for the other channels you're welcome to add. You will find topics there such as: Canvas LMS, introductions, worklifebalance, assessment, specs grading, etc.

Thank you, again, for getting in touch.

Text expansion programs work in the vast majority of computer programs, including word processors, spreadsheets, web browsers, and email clients. Text expansion applications can help answer commonly asked questions over email; keep date and other formats consistent; and have various kinds of email signatures, based on different roles or professional identities.

I use TextExpander as my text expansion application. It is simple to set up snippets. TextExpander tracks how much time it has saved me in the last month, how many snippets it has expanded, and the most frequently used snippets. Using TextExpander means no more spending time looking up information (e.g., phone numbers, email addresses), and no more having to copy/paste commonly used text from a template.

When I want to add a new snippet, I open the TextExpander application and press the + button to enter the shortcut (snippet) I want to use and the associated text to be expanded. Snippets can be grouped in folders and kept organized within the TextExpander application.

Basic Uses of Text Expansion

Getting started with a text expansion application is relatively easy. You create an account, especially if you want your snippets to be available to you on multiple computers and/or devices. Then, you determine how you will structure your snippets. TextExpander experts typically use some unusual character to indicate the start of a snippet, followed by a single word or abbreviation. David Sparks of the Mac Power Users uses an *x* as the start of his snippet words. For example, he has *xcell* translate into his cell phone number. My starting character for TextExpander snippets is generally the letter *z*. For example, I have *zzoom* expand into the link for my Zoom web conference meeting room.

Here are some examples of small ways I got started creating snippets, and these are the ones I wound up using most frequently:

- Email addresses (e.g., *d@il* results in my husband's email address)
- Signatures (e.g., *vusig* results in my Vanguard University signature)
- Phone numbers (e.g., *zvuphone* results in my Vanguard University phone number)
- Web links (e.g., *linkofficehours* results in the URL to my web-based office hours scheduling tool)

My Most Common Uses of TextExpander

It is hard to imagine working on a computer that did not have TextExpander installed on it. I have also installed TextExpander on my iPhone and iPad, to be able to use my snippets, even when I am not on my primary computer. Fortunately, I do not have to guess what my most common uses of TextExpander are. The application provides statistics that indicate my most often used snippets:

- *Various signatures*: I teach as an adjunct at one institution and am a resident faculty member at another, along with being the dean of teaching and learning. Finally, I have a signature related to the

Teaching in Higher Ed podcast, which I use when getting in touch with potential guests or people who contact me about the show.

- *Slack group information*: I have a community for the *Teaching in Higher Ed* podcast on Slack. I generally get one or two sign-up requests per day. Having a TextExpander snippet means I only have to click on the requester's email address to start a reply, type a subject line for the email, and then activate the text to inform the person that I have added them to the Slack group and encourage them to customize the nonstandard channels.
- *Zoom link*: I teach online using the Zoom web-conferencing platform, as well as leverage it for plenty of meetings and other means of communication. I have a snippet that enters the link to my meeting room.
- *Show notes*: I have a template for my podcast's show notes that uses a fill-in snippet to ask me for the podcast guest's name, the episode number, and other information about the upcoming episode. It inputs all the variables into the text and produces a customized template for me to use for the show notes.

Leveraging Others' TextExpander Snippets

The TextExpander website offers groups that contain collections of snippets that you can download and add to your TextExpander. Some of the collections are to correct common typos through autocorrect (*sentance* becomes *sentence, questionaire* becomes *questionnaire, teh* becomes *the*, etc.). These snippets are refined over time by an editor and therefore keep improving.

You can also find TextExpander snippets on individuals' blogs. Sparks (n.d.) has a collection of snippets on his MacSparky website. He has snippets for meeting notes, conference calls, OmniFocus, Markdown, and date-and-time-related snippets. Schmitz (2014) outlines on the Asian Efficiency site how he is even able to put a snippet inside another snippet.

PRODUCTIVE GRADING

Productivity in grading can be elusive. We want to provide valuable feedback to our students, yet the realities of our workloads can be overwhelming. It can lead us to feel discouraged about just how much effort to put into the process of grading.

We want to see that our grading shapes students' learning and we can often be left without perceiving the value in our investment of time. Haswell (1983) determined that correcting every single instance of a mistake in our grading does not improve students' writing. Instead, he developed a method where he marks errors with a check mark in the margin in the same line as the location of the error. In the case of 2 errors in the same line, he includes 2 check marks. Then, he returns the papers 15 minutes before the end of class and has students make the corrections themselves and resubmit their papers. He states, "Until a student attempts to correct checked errors, the grade on the essay remains unrecorded" (p. 601).

Haswell's (1983) method could easily be transferred to the digital realm. Check marks can be made using a stylus with a tablet, or a stamp of a check mark, available in many LMS grading systems and PDF annotating applications.

The overall focus on grading writing assignments should not be to catch and correct every error, but to be sure we are giving students ample opportunities for practice, which requires that we provide useful feedback. "Just as we teach children how to ride bikes by putting them on a bicycle, we need to teach students how to write grammatically by letting them write" (Navarre-Cleary, 2014, para. 5).

My approach to grading is to automate where possible to free up more of my time for providing qualitative and more personalized feedback. In many cases, this translates to having an established rubric that articulates the primary grading components of the assignment along with the associated number of points related to the criteria. Some find rubrics too constraining, both concerning having students take a more creative approach to how they produce their assignments and also in giving faculty an opportunity to provide rich feedback during the grading process.

Using Rubrics

Rubrics help save me time because I avoid repeating the same criteria that were articulated in the assignment description regarding what was expected. However, it

We want to see that our grading shapes students' learning.

#ThriveOnline

does not provide feedback as individualized as I think my students deserve. That makes it more of a starting point for me. The book *Introduction to Rubrics: An Assessment Tool to Save Grading Time, Convey Effective Feedback, and Promote Student Learning* (Stevens, Levi, & Walvoord, 2012) provides a wonderful way to get started with this method of feedback. The Association of American Colleges & Universities (2014) has 16 Valid Assessment of Learning in Undergraduate Education (VALUE) rubrics that you can customize to gauge student work within a liberal education context.

Specifications Grading

A theme that has been emphasized throughout this book is being more efficient with some tasks to free up time for the more important activities. When it comes to grading, professors aim to make the logistical part of grading easier in order to have ample opportunities to provide rich feedback. One of these approaches is known as specifications grading.

Nilson (2014) stresses that grading is unnecessarily complicated and does not effectively articulate whether a student has acquired the necessary competencies being assessed. Advocates for specifications grading approach their assignments in a binary way. Students either met the expectations or they did not. They are able to refine their work and resubmit it, allowing the focus to be on the learning that comes from an iterative process. The feedback provided to students is directly related to helping them meet the requirements for the assignment, and time does not need to be spent justifying why the student's grade was a B+ instead of an A.

Video and Screencast Feedback

Another technique I use to save time and provide richer feedback to students is video. If the assignment could benefit from a more personalized approach to feedback, I will sometimes record a video of myself using my webcam. This allows the students to see my facial expressions and hear the inflections in my voice.

In other cases, I record a video of my screen (known as screencasting) with students' assignments in view during the recording. This approach helps direct the learners' attention back to the portions of their work that are being discussed. I am also able to bring up other items on the screen during the recording to note other resources that may be helpful in extending the learning.

Researchers explored the effectiveness of video feedback on assessments by analyzing 126 students' perceptions. They asked for the students' reactions to 5-minute videos that were recorded by their professors. Students reported that they found the feedback more "individualized (specific) and personalized (valorizing identity and effort); supportive, caring and motivating; clear, detailed and unambiguous; prompting reflection; and constructive, which led to future strategizing" (Henderson & Phillips, 2015, p. 51). Video-based feedback can not only save time during the grading process but also significantly benefit the students.

The Canvas LMS has the capability to screencast feedback to students from within the SpeedGrader tool. When using LMSs without that feature, it is easy to include screencasted videos using tools such as Droplr, Screencast-O-Matic, Studio, or Snagit. See the appendix for other options.

TAKE ACTION: LEVERAGING TECHNOLOGY TOWARD GREATER PRODUCTIVITY

This is an opportunity to reflect on which steps are most important to take after reading through Part Four. Here are specific next actions you may want to record in your task manager or in a someday/maybe list to increase the impact of the book:

❑ Consider using batch processing in some aspect of your work. Set up a context in your task management system for accomplishing tasks that all require the same tools to complete in a batch. An easy way to start this process is to set up a context for your LMS and record each task that needs to be done the next time you're online and logged in.

❑ Create a checklist for the start of a new term or a new academic year. Review Gawande's (2010) checklist on checklists and modify your checklist as needed.

❑ Compose a checklist for each time you onboard a TA or graduate student or other repetitive series of tasks that can be made more seamless with a checklist.

- ❏ Build a form for when students want to request a reference or letter of recommendation from you.
- ❏ Explore IFTTT or Zapier for ways that they may help you in automating some aspect of your work.
- ❏ Visit the Thrive Online website at thriveonlineseries .com to discover other ways to have more significant grading productivity.
- ❏ Share on #ThriveOnline what technology you are experimenting with to boost your productivity.

PART FIVE

KEEPING CURRENT

KEEPING CURRENT

How do we keep other parts of our online courses current and make updating as easy as possible? In this part, we consider ways to approach updating courses that are stored in an LMS. We also look at essential data and file management techniques as well as cloud computing.

The major LMSs today have built-in mechanisms for making content management and updating more efficient. While it is not feasible to include a breakdown of every LMS, explore the techniques described in this part to know what features to search for on the tools that you use. Approaches that will work on any LMS (or similar platform) are featured in the upcoming sections to provide the most substantial impact in keeping our content, dates, and other variables current.

There is still a considerable amount of our work that exists outside the LMS itself. In instructional design circles, these files are known as assets. A slide deck, quiz, video, or syllabus is an asset that we will use in constructing our online course and in populating it with learning resources. Being able to locate files easily is vital to our productivity. Otherwise, we will spend more time searching for assets than creating them and sharing them with our students. Another aspect in keeping current is planning for the inevitable technical woes that can destroy years of work if we have not made backups or taken other preventive measures.

Pacheco-Vega (2016) reminds us how not having an organized system for keeping current can hinder our productivity:

> This problem happens to all of us: we have a number of things that need processing (committee materials, student files, printouts, etc.). Often times, we are so overwhelmed by other things that we end up saying "oh, I'll file these materials soon" and end up needing to have accessed them before. (para. 1)

Part Five is about how to keep the content we store in the LMS current and to find what we are looking for on our computers and cloud storage services. We also explore how to stay more productive and secure using a password manager and avoid the significant time it takes to troubleshoot security issues when an account is compromised.

A PKM system becomes personal when we include resources that will be relevant because of our strengths, our interests, and our motivations.

#ThriveOnline

INSIDE THE LMS

It can be challenging to keep course content and date-related items in an LMS current. If just one link to a resource is broken, or a date is set to the last time the course was taught, it can result in multiple confused and concerned emails from students, wasting numerous people's time. Felix (2003) articulates the importance of keeping the content within an LMS current:

> [The LMS] can provide a valuable service to students, by centralizing a variety of electronic resources and tools which aid learning and communication. Instructors should keep in mind that if they expect students to use the [course] site on a regular basis, they themselves need to do so as well, keeping the content current and informative. (p. 53)

Continuous Improvement

The most basic way to save time in updating course content is to make a change as soon as you notice an error. That way, it will be corrected for any students who have yet to access that portion of the course. As students share resources that they have found helpful in discussion boards, over email, or via social media, consider adding those links to the primary course shell so they can be available for the next course. A more sophisticated way of doing this is to establish a course wiki, which provides a method for multiple people to collaborate and share resources.

Wikis are websites that are constructed and maintained by many users instead of by a single author. The most famous wiki, of course, is Wikipedia. However, the ability to quickly add and edit information in a collaborative way is possible on a much smaller scale. Some LMSs have wiki capabilities built inside their platforms, and some faculty use wiki websites to build out their class wiki pages.

Course Date Adjustments

Keeping dates current for quizzes, exams, papers, and other assignments can be a challenge. The good news is that most LMSs can adjust course dates when copying a course over to a new term, which also adjusts deadlines for assignment within a class. If a quiz is due the Friday of the second week of class, the LMS asks what date the new course term begins and adjusts the date accordingly. It is well worth getting in touch with a resident LMS expert to inquire whether your LMS has this feature. Typing in a start date and an end date for a term and letting the system work its magic is way more efficient than having to enter each and every due date by hand.

RSS Content and Widgets

Content can be kept current within an LMS by subscribing to feeds that are contained outside the LMS. Laura Gibbs, an online instructor at the University of Oklahoma, provides an example of this technique. She uses the Canvas LMS and subscribes to feeds from WordPress, YouTube,

Pinterest, Twitter, Google+, Flickr, and her social book-marking tool of choice (Diigo).

Instead of having to update the LMS each time she adds a video on YouTube, Gibbs (n.d.) just adds the video to the relevant playlist on YouTube and never has to change a thing within her LMS. Within the LMS, she has linked to a playlist, instead of to specific video files. Then, any videos that get added to the playlist on YouTube automatically show up for students when they are inside the course site.

The same concept applies when Gibbs posts a new bookmark link on Diigo. She teaches a fables course and may add a new bookmark related to her stories from India. Instead of needing to post that same link on the LMS, it shows up automatically. Gibbs subscribes to an RSS feed of her bookmarks on Diigo that are related to her fables course. Any time new bookmarks are added they get updated and "fed" over to her course within the LMS.

FILE MANAGEMENT TECHNIQUES

Taking time to locate files is an unproductive activity. Documents should be easy to locate. We also want to avoid using any problematic characters that could inadvertently cause issues when sending the file to someone else or when trying to import the data into different applications. Finally, being consistent with our naming conventions allows us to spend less time coming up with what to name a given file.

As pointed out by VanMouwerik (2016), having an organized file management system is an integral part of any productivity system. She emphasizes, "Cleaning up your computer is just the first step in the process of building a sustainable and efficient organization system" (para. 20). The following sections discuss how to name files using dates without causing problems, avoid problematic characters, troubleshoot, and organize files related to teaching.

Date References

Many people always include the date in a file name, whether or not that information is necessary. One way to avoid redundant work is to avoid using date references in files that do not warrant them. Sometimes people include the date that a file was created in the file name, not realizing that the information can be culled from the file's metadata. Information such as when a file was created, when it was last modified, and the author is stored within the document itself. If you click on any file on your computer and then press either control-i (on Windows) or command-i (on a Mac), you will be able to view the metadata for the file, including the date that the file was created and when it was last modified.

If date references are imperative for a given file, start with the year in the file name, followed by either month-day or day-month, depending on what is standard ordering in your region. For example, if I had a bimonthly update on student metrics, I would call it this:

2021-09-01-student-metrics-update

That way, when I have a bunch of student metrics updates, they will be listed in an easy-to-comprehend order, such as the following:

2021-09-01-student-metrics-update
2021-10-01-student-metrics-update
2021-11-01-student-metrics-update
2021-12-01-student-metrics-update
2021-13-01-student-metrics-update

The leading zeros (09 versus 9) enable the files to remain listed by date. The single-digit months (January 01 through September 09) do not disrupt the date order.

Year/Semester References

It can be useful to distinguish between files that are related to course content and those documents that are specific to a particular semester. For example, a PowerPoint file on chapter 1 that I use in my introduction to business class (BUSN114) is named busn114-ppt-ch1.pptx. For that same class, a PowerPoint submitted by a student on the industry analysis assignment is named 2019f-busn114-industry-smith-marco.

It is helpful to consider the order in which you list the information within the file names, given the default ways that computer operating systems sort files. By adding the year/semester reference to the beginning of a file name, I can ensure that all files from that same semester will be listed together when I am viewing them or performing a search that pulls up year/semester-specific information.

Problematic Characters

Having separators in file names is a helpful way to discern the contents of a document. However, some of the separators that people use in file names wind up being problematic down the road. Following is a list of characters to avoid when attempting to separate characters in a file name, along with the reason why the character can cause issues:

- *Forward slashes*: Back in the days when computer operating systems did not have graphical user interfaces, they used to be made up entirely of text. We used to use forward slashes to separate file names from where they were stored (e.g., drive/directory/file.txt). If we name a file 2018/09/01/update, its possible that there will not be any problems. However, depending on where this information is stored, we might end up confusing the system we are using. A computer might interpret that our update is stored inside a folder called 2018, instead of reading a single file name. Therefore, it is best to use nonambiguous separators for dates and other information within a file name.
- *Periods*: Another challenging character to use in a file name is a period. Files on computer systems contain what are called extensions. They are at the end of a file name, and they let the computer know

what program to use to open the file. For example, a file ending in .docx means that the file has the extension for a Microsoft Word document. When double clicking on the file name, the .docx tells the operating system that the kind of file attempting to be opened is a Microsoft Word file, so it never even asks you what program to use. When periods are used in a file name, it can confuse a computer operating system. It might think that there is some new kind of program it never heard of before but is supposed to use to open the file. When viewing documents on a computer, these extensions (the period with the extra characters that indicate the file types) may not always be visible. For example, on a Mac, the view may be set to leave off extensions, for people who prefer a simpler look.

- *Spaces*: Today's computer operating systems do not typically have a problem with spaces. However, storing files with spaces in their name somewhere that they might be accessed on the Internet can be a challenge. For example, syllabi are commonly shared from a cloud storage service such as Dropbox or OneDrive or uploaded to an LMS. Web links cannot contain spaces. Instead, most systems translate spaces into a special character, most commonly %. While links that include % will undoubtedly work, they do tend to make for less attractive web links than other options do.

Michigan Tech (n.d.) lists other problematic characters that should be avoided (Figure 5.1).

Figure 5.1. Characters to avoid in file names.

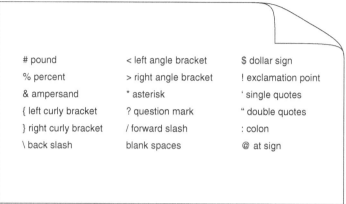

# pound	< left angle bracket	$ dollar sign
% percent	> right angle bracket	! exclamation point
& ampersand	* asterisk	' single quotes
{ left curly bracket	? question mark	" double quotes
} right curly bracket	/ forward slash	: colon
\ back slash	blank spaces	@ at sign

A Useful Separator

Oregon State University (n.d.) recommends dashes as file name separators, even above the other commonly used separator of an underscore. Although an underscore is not likely to cause technical issues, if an underscore appears in a hyperlink, which is indicated by an underline, it can be difficult to see that there are two lines because they overlap. Using a dash where you might otherwise have had a space, forward slash, or period in a file name gives the advantage of greater readability of file names without any of the issues we have discussed regarding the other types of separators.

Here are a few examples of how dashes can be used in file names:

busn114-ch01.pptx
productive-online-professor-proposal-v4.docs
book-mockup.pptx

Note that when creating the example files, I never typed in the .pptx. That happened automatically after I provided the main file name and then saved it. Again, depending on your settings, you may or may not see the last part of the file name. Rest assured, it is there, even if it is hidden.

Numbers in File Names

When previously describing how to use date references in a file name, I explained the benefits of having the year first in the file name. Other techniques help with the long-term goal of making files easier to locate. When using numbers in file names, consider how you might want them to be ordered when viewing a list of files. Use zeros in front of single-digit chapter numbers, for example, to avoid a list like this:

busn114-ch1.pptx
busn114-ch10.pptx
busn114-ch11.pptx
busn114-ch2.pptx
busn114-ch3.pptx
busn114-ch4.pptx
busn114-ch5.pptx
busn114-ch6.pptx
busn114.ch7.pptx
busn114.ch8.pptx
busn114.ch9.pptx

Placing a zero in front of the first chapter will keep your chapters in order, as follows:

busn114-ch01.pptx
busn114-ch02.pptx
busn114-ch03.pptx

If you have a numbering scheme that will ultimately exceed two digits, add two zeros in front of your file names (e.g., update-001.pptx).

Case Sensitivity

There are instances where having capital letters in file names will not cause issues. However, as Oregon State University (n.d.) reminds us, the element of case "can potentially affect both computer performance, as well as human usability" (para. 7).

When transferring files or folders to a different platform (e.g., moving a file online), using capital letters can go from being fine to suddenly causing files to be overwritten or making them difficult to locate. My-Slides is viewed as different from my-slides on the Internet, but not when using Windows. Using all lowercase letters in your file names will mean that when you move files between your primary computer to somewhere on the Internet you will not have to worry about experiencing difficulties.

Lost Files

I spent the first 10 years of my career in the computer training industry. An introduction to computers course in the early 1990s might include objectives such as how to create, edit, and delete folders. This often came before the participants ever even learned how to create a document. Where we stored our files and how we set up that structure used to make quite a difference in our ability to navigate in our computing life.

I frequently meet students who have no idea where their files are on their computers. The recent files list that is offered in most applications provides them with a sufficient means to access and put the finishing touches on the paper they have recently worked on. However, after they submit their paper, they move on to the next one and never look back.

The challenge, of course, arises when people need to go back to a file that they worked on more than a year ago. Where did that document go? Because it is no longer listed in the recently opened files within the application it was created in, people often find themselves desperately trying to locate a document that is suddenly important to them once again.

The Desktop Dilemma

Some people avoid folders entirely and store everything on their desktop. On Windows and Mac, the desktop is the main screen you see when you first start your computer, or when no programs are currently open. Files can be stored on the desktop, making it easy to see them, just as leaving papers we are working on out on our desk makes it easier to see them than if they were in a drawer.

However, the desktop can quickly become cluttered, making it very difficult to find our files. The desktop is also a folder on our computers. If you open the folders that are stored on your computer, you will see one called "Desktop," which contains everything that is currently on your desktop. On a Mac, you can view all the folders and files on your computer by opening up the finder. On a PC, your directory structure can be seen by opening Windows Explorer.

Search Versus Folders

There are two primary methods for addressing the issue of lost files. Search has become so powerful on computing devices that it is possible to have a single folder where files are kept and to rely on search to locate a document. However, most computer users prefer the second method, which is to set up a directory structure (set of folders) to provide at least some level of organization.

In any given semester, there are two folders where I spend most of my digital time: a semester-specific folder and a course-specific folder. As with my file-naming methodology described previously, these folders are used to keep files separate that relate to a particular class (regardless of when I teach it) and that relate to a specific semester (and the students' coursework from those classes I am teaching that term).

Semester-Specific Folder

Each time I begin preparing for a new semester to start, I create a folder to store all the work products that will be produced in that time period. Here is an example of what these folders might look like if viewed in list format:

2020f
2021s
2021su
2021f
2022s

I have been teaching for more than 15 years now, so you can imagine that the list of semesters could get pretty long and clutter up an otherwise clean directory structure. Therefore, I have a folder named "z-archive" that I drag older semesters into once all the work for a given semester has closed out (grades have been entered, etc.). The *z* at the start of the folder name is a technique I use to ensure that it always stays at the bottom of any list in which it appears. If I did not include the *z*, the *a* in *archive* would cause it to be closer to the top of the list instead.

Within a given semester-specific folder, I include the following types of files:

- *Semester schedule*: This file contains an Excel spreadsheet (also saved as a PDF) with my semester's schedule, along with office hours and other schedule information that would be relevant to students.
- *Ideal week schedule*: I design an ideal week schedule each semester, which is modeled after a methodology developed by Michael Hyatt (2011), former CEO of Thomas Nelson Publishing, which we discussed in Part One.
- *Textbook adoptions*: Our university's bookstore requires that we submit an Excel spreadsheet

that contains all our course textbooks for a given semester.

- *Semester forms and/or agreements*: We are required to fill out a form each semester that confirms what classes we are teaching, any overload classes we have taken on, and what committee work we are performing that semester.
- *Rosters*: I have rosters for each course I am teaching in a given semester. If it is an in-person course, I use these as sign-in sheets. In the case of online classes, I use them to take attendance during our synchronous sessions (and to track whom I have yet to ask a question of and invite the person to engage).

Course-Specific Folder

Inside each of the course-specific folders, I have a folder for every assignment within that semester. My consumer behavior course has the following file structure:

- *Course reserves*: Any library resources that have been requested/made available are generated through an Excel form. I keep a copy of the filled-out form for my records.
- *Midterm feedback*: I keep the information gleaned from my midterm course feedback, which allows me to take action on this input as the class progresses.

Inside each of the course-specific folders, I also have a folder for each assignment within that semester. My consumer behavior course might have the following file structure:

1-development-opportunity-1
2-development-opportunity-2
3-development-opportunity-3
4-development-opportunity-4
5-reflection-papers
6-poster-sessions

I do not always use that many course-specific folders, instead relying on the LMS to archive students' work for me. In the past, being able to access prior students' work without having to dig through the LMS has been an easier approach, but there are a lot of variables as to whether or not I keep the students' papers and other assignments on my computer.

Favorites

A crucial part of my digital organizational system involves the use of favorites. On both a Mac and a PC, you can identify some of your folders as favorites. They then show up on the left-hand side of your list of files/folders and on the left-hand side of the window when you are saving files.

I keep the following folders on my favorites list:

- Primary course-specific folder: 1-courses
- Semester-specific folder: 2020f
- Main Teaching in Higher Ed folder: teaching-in-higher-ed
- Folders for projects that I am currently working on

There are too many variables involved to provide precise information on how to create favorites on all variations of the various operating systems. However, a quick Google search on, for example, how to add folders to favorites on Windows (whatever version of Windows you are using) will lead you to the information you need.

Invitation to Connect

Have you struggled to find a document on your computer and wound up wasting time in the search or eventually given up and had to recreate it? How can you use one of the approaches discussed in this chapter to avoid wasting time in the future looking for files? Share your thoughts using #ThriveOnline.

CLOUD COMPUTING

When I taught computer classes in the early 1990s, we stressed the importance of structuring one's hard drive similar to how you might structure a hard-copy filing system. Now, there are many reasons to consider storing our files somewhere besides our hard drive and making use of so-called cloud computing.

When a file is stored in the cloud, it is being stored on someone else's computer (called a server), instead of (or in addition to) on a local hard drive. Technically speaking, you are actually storing files on a system built with an extensive network of servers that are all interconnected. There is not a literal cloud somewhere in the sky, but rather large warehouses filled with servers that are kept cool and secure.

A couple of years ago, a colleague's computer was stolen out of her office during the lunch hour. She had kept all of her files related to her teaching, research, and the group she was an adviser for all on that same computer. Years of her work were gone in an instant. The only files she was ever able to recover were those that were stored on our LMS within her old class shells, or the files that were kept by her departmental assistant.

Keeping files only locally on a hard drive is risky business. When it comes to our productivity, it can all come to a screeching halt if we lose access to our files. If I store my course syllabus solely on my hard drive, for example, I could run into the following issues:

- My hard drive fails, and I am unable to retrieve files from it.
- I am in a department meeting and need to reference my syllabus but do not have my computer with me.
- After having sent my syllabus to our program coordinator, I realize I made a mistake and have to resend the file (versus that update happening automatically).

Cloud file storage is most often preferable to solely storing files locally on a hard drive. To access a file that is stored on the cloud, you only need an Internet connection. That means you can open that file on your smartphone, on a tablet, or even on someone else's computer. When you make changes to the file on your computer, those changes get synced over to the cloud service, ensuring that modifications are kept consistent within that file, regardless of what device you used to open it.

Years of her work were gone in an instant.

#ThriveOnline

Many cloud services give you the ability to work offline, meaning that even having an Internet connection is not essential at all times. I use a cloud service called Dropbox. There is a Dropbox folder on my computer, which houses almost all the files I keep on my hard drive, but this same folder is replicated online and can be accessed on my many devices, or anywhere I can get an Internet connection (public library, coffee shop, etc.).

If I am traveling, or am otherwise without an Internet connection, I can just open the files and work on them as I would normally from my computer. When my Internet connection is restored, all changes are made, and my cloud-based files become current once again.

Selecting a Cloud Service

Deciding which cloud service to use can be complex. The good news is that the choices are abundant and the prices keep coming down. At a minimum, be sure any cloud service you use has these features:

- Connects with whatever computing ecosystem you are on (e.g., if you use a Mac, the system must work on Macs)
- Works on whatever mobile devices you use
- Allows you to view/download older versions of a file, in case you want to go back to how the file looked before you accidentally saved over it
- Has a stellar reputation when it comes to security and privacy
- Complies with institutional/country regulations on cloud storage

Invitation to Connect

What cloud service do you use and what do you like the most about it? Share your experiences using #ThriveOnline.

Other Considerations

One of the other significant advantages of cloud services is collaboration. If your institution uses Microsoft OneDrive, for example, it makes sense to adopt it because then you will be able to more easily share files with others and make changes that all sync back into the same document. I use Dropbox for the majority of my course files, as well as in collaboration with our podcast editor. However, when working with colleagues at my primary institution, I choose OneDrive because that is what has been adopted for cloud storage for the campus.

Before committing to storing everything on your institution's cloud service, be aware that in many instances your privacy could be legally compromised. Employment law generally dictates that if you are using a computer (and associated services) that were purchased by the organization, they can view your files. Some institutions have policies that negate this general practice, in the interest of academic freedom and values about privacy. However, be advised that you are safest if you keep personal files on a cloud service account that is not being provided by your employer, regardless of what has been articulated in policy. My advice is to identify any personal files you have stored on your employer-sponsored cloud service and transfer them to an account/service that you pay for.

A Cautionary Note About Backups

When people discover cloud services, they often stop worrying about having backups of their files. Although some cloud services include some aspect of backup, it is considered a good practice to have multiple methods of backup. I back up all my files using these methods:

- Whatever cloud service I am using for a particular task, most often Dropbox
- My backup service (Backblaze)
- Apple's Time Machine backup technology (stores my files on an external hard drive to which my Mac connects)

Relying on only one means of backup, and particularly a service that is not designed to be a backup service, is a risk not worth taking. It is best if we ensure that we have at least a couple of ways our data are protected, in case technology woes come our way.

As Cavender (2016a) stresses:

Rules of computing:

1. If it's important, back it up.
2. Refer to Rule #3.
3. See Rule #1. (para. 1)

Those are serious rules. Really. There's nothing more horrifying than losing the only copy of something you've spent hours/days/weeks/months on.

I was on Twitter recently and saw someone talking about how she had just lost three years of work on her dissertation because her computer had been stolen. While backups are hardly the first thing people talk about in terms of being productive professors, all it takes is one time losing a bunch of work on something major to discover how much of a waste of time not having a system in place can potentially be.

LINKING SMART

Consider all the places where a syllabus may appear. It may be posted on an LMS, sent to an assistant for the department's records, posted on a website, or sent to an individual student who has inquired about the required textbooks in advance of the semester. The challenge comes into play when changes get made to the syllabus after it has been posted or sent. All the places to which the syllabus has been distributed are difficult to track down to provide an updated file. It can also be challenging to determine whether someone is referencing the most current version.

Prestopnik (2015) is keenly aware of the challenge of having multiple versions of a file posted in an LMS and not having a robust organizational system when presenting learning resources for students. He provides the following example:

> If you post your course syllabus or any other file or content in multiple locations throughout your course site, that is inviting error. When you go to

> update the content, to make a slight clarification, change a date, etc., you now must update that content in several locations throughout your course site. Can you even remember everywhere you placed that content? (para. 4)

Instead of relying on sending out the actual file to the various recipients or posting it on an LMS, it is far more effective to post or send a link to the file after it has been posted on a cloud storage system, such as Dropbox, Google Drive, or Microsoft's OneDrive. As changes are made to the file, the link to the file remains current. The next time students go to their email message, or to the LMS where the link to the syllabus has been provided, they will be accessing the most current version. Students should be made aware of big changes to a syllabus such as due date changes or modifications to the point system. However, minor changes do not always warrant notifying students, and it is far easier to have everyone know that the most current version of the file will always be located via the link on the LMS or within the email message.

When managing these types of documents, the goal is always to be able to access older versions of course syllabi and know what term/semester each document refers to without having to open the file. We can accomplish this by doing a save-as on the course syllabus word-processing file from the last time we taught it and by giving the new file a semester-specific file name.

Another goal in managing syllabi is to avoid having to reupload a new syllabus to the LMS each time we start

As changes are made to the file, the link to the file remains current.

#ThriveOnline

a new term/semester. We want one version of the current syllabus in PDF format that does not have a date-specific file name so that any places where we have linked to the file remain intact and do not have to be updated each time. If students have already downloaded the PDF file to their computer, the updated file will not automatically get changed within the PDF that is already on their computer. While it does present a potential flaw in this system, this would still be the case if they had been initially sent the actual file (versus a link to the file) in the first place.

Save Archives of Each Syllabus in Microsoft Word Format

Let's use an introduction to business course (BUSN114) being taught in the spring semester of 2021 as an example of how to archive each syllabus. The last time the professor taught the course was in the fall of 2020. The professor provided the following unique file name to indicate the semester the course was being taught:

busn114-2020f.docx

Each time a new semester's preparation begins, the previous class's syllabus is opened and a save-as is done. When the spring of 2021 comes up, the busn114-2020f.docx remains intact, and the save-as command allows the file to be renamed for the new semester as follows:

busn114-2021s.docs

Save the Syllabus as a PDF With No Date References

To avoid circulating or posting a Word file, when all changes and edits have been made, save the file as a PDF but without the date-specific information. Using the previous BUSN114 example, we would name the file as follows:

busn114.pdf

Regardless of how many semesters the course is taught, only one PDF file ever remains in the folder of syllabi. That is the only file that ever gets linked to in the various services (LMS, website, etc.) and the only file that ever gets distributed out to departmental assistants and students who may be thinking about the coming semester.

In the case of BUSN114, if this class was taught previously, the folder with syllabi will already contain a file from the previous time the course was taught. When the new semester's syllabus is saved as a PDF, a dialog box asking whether or not to replace the original file will be presented. Choose to replace the original file and all the places where the old file was linked to will then be updated to reflect the most current information. The sharing link to the file remains the same, while the text that is inside it has been changed to reflect the new dates for the term/semester, as well as any other information that has been changed for the upcoming class.

During a semester in which four classes are being taught, the syllabi folder would contain the following files:

```
institution/syllabi/
busn114-2020f.docx
busn114.pdf
mrkt360-2020f.docx
mrkt360.pdf
mrkt366-2020f.docx
mrkt366.pdf
mrkt369-2020f.docx
mrkt369.pdf
z-archive
```

It is important to keep these PDF files in the same place as they were used to link to in the past, or the links that have been established will be broken. The Word documents (.docx) can be moved into an archive folder, once the semester is over, as described in the next section.

Maintain an Archive Folder for Older Syllabi

Notice that at the bottom of the syllabi folder in the previous section is a folder named z-archive. The letter *z* is at the front of the file name so it will be listed at the bottom of the list of files—assuming they are sorted in alphabetical order. Each time a new semester starts, the older syllabus can be opened, saved as a new version to reflect the date-specific information for the coming semester, and then the older word-processing file can be moved into the z-archive folder.

Share Links to Syllabi and Other Files Versus Actual Files

In the previous sections we described the process of keeping an archive of syllabi saved in word-processing format. We also explored saving those word-processing documents as PDFs but removing any date-specific information from the file names. Each time a new semester's syllabi are finished being modified, the edited files are saved in PDF documents. When we are in the process of saving them as PDFs, the dialog box asks whether or not to replace the old PDF file, and the answer is a resounding "yes." The older version still exists in the word-processing format, but the PDF version remains as always the most current edition—and the one that has been linked all over the place.

This section describes various ways of sharing links to files. Cloud storage services can be accessed via a web browser. Whether the preferred cloud option is Dropbox, Apple's iCloud, Google Drive, Box, or Microsoft's One-Drive, it is possible to log in to their service on your web browser and have a way of viewing all files. Once a file that is to be shared is located, identify whether to let the recipient view the file or to be able to edit it.

When linking to syllabi, the majority of the time the most appropriate option is to share a public link to the file, but not one that allows for editing of the file. In Dropbox, choose share, and then select the option to create a link to the file (if this link has not already been created and posted within the LMS in the past).

It can sometimes be cumbersome to have to open up a web browser to copy a share link for a given file. Instead, some of the cloud services have an application that can run on a computer and produce share links from within the familiar file management interface we are accustomed to using. Dropbox, for example, creates a folder on the user's hard drive when the user installs its service. That is where the files go that are then synced over to the Dropbox service. A copy then exists on not only the user's hard drive but also Dropbox's servers. Any changes that get made in either place are synced to all devices (smartphone, tablet, computer, and the browser) where Dropbox is installed.

When using Dropbox and sharing a syllabus, you simply open the Dropbox folder and navigate to where the PDF of the syllabus is kept. Next you right-click on the syllabus PDF and choose "copy Dropbox link." The link is placed in the clipboard, where it stays until it gets pasted somewhere (or something else gets copied and replaces it). You then paste the resulting link in all the places where the syllabus is needed, such as within the LMS, in an email to whoever should receive it, or onto a website.

Visit the Thrive Online website at thriveonlineseries .com to see a video of this process in action.

Other Alternatives

The method described for handling syllabi file management assumes that an actual file is needed to distribute the syllabus information. If that assumption proves false, the syllabus verbiage could be included on a page

Visit the Thrive
Online website at
thriveonlineseries.com
to see a video of how to
link smart.

#ThriveOnline

right within the LMS, meaning that any updates would be instantaneous on the LMS page and there would be no concerns about an out-of-date version existing on a student's computer. If creating and maintaining pages within the LMS is problematic, the syllabus could be stored on a cloud-based writing app, such as Google Docs or Dropbox Paper. Then, the resulting syllabus could be linked to or embedded from within the LMS.

PASSWORD MANAGERS

Having secure passwords for all your accounts is an aspect of productivity that is often not considered until it is too late. If our accounts are hacked, we can spend an inordinate amount of time cleaning up the mess, not to mention putting our students' information at risk.

Within the top 10 industries that have experienced data breaches, higher education ranks third. These security break-ins were determined to be caused by "weak, default, or stolen passwords" 63% of the time (Keeper Security, 2016, para. 3).

Reusing the same password for different websites puts us at risk of having multiple accounts broken into within a short duration. Once an unscrupulous person has information on the login we use for one website, that person might have the data needed to break into our email, and then reset even those passwords that we have set up to be more secure, such as those for our banking and other payment services.

Each website gets its own password.

#ThriveOnline

Common Features

A password manager allows you to remember only a single password to then access secure passwords for all your accounts. Each website gets its own password. When logging into a bank website, we press the button for our password manager within our web browser, and it enters the secure password for us.

Coming up with secure passwords can be difficult. Password managers can perform that function for us as well. We tell it what "recipe" we want it to use (e.g., the login needs to have a certain number of special characters), and it comes up with a secure password that we can copy and paste over into the new service we are signing up for. It also then saves that login information for future times we access the same site.

These services can also store other vital information, such as the following:

- Credit card data
- Social Security numbers
- Passport photos
- Wireless router configurations
- Software licenses
- Identities (with addresses, phone numbers, email addresses, etc., that can be entered with two clicks in a website that is inquiring about that data)
- Driver's licenses

If your computer or other device is stolen, the thief would be unable to get inside your password manager unless they know your primary password (which you would be wise to keep absolutely secure because it is what keeps you protected). The individual passwords that you keep inside the manager are encrypted, so even the company that makes the software is unable to have access to your information. Encryption is a process of mixing up the letters, numbers, words, and symbols in a database and having only the "key" to put the pieces of the puzzle back together again be stored by the authorized party. In this case, the person with your primary password is the only person with that key to unencrypt the information.

Two popular password managers worth looking into are 1Password and LastPass. Although no system is 100% secure, password managers help us decrease the likelihood that someone will gain access to information that will hurt us financially or take up our precious time having to try to take back our data. As Hoffman (2018) reminds us, "A password manager will take a load off your mind, freeing up brain power for doing productive things rather than remembering a long list of passwords" (para. 6).

TAKE ACTION: KEEPING CURRENT

This is an opportunity to reflect on which steps are most important to take after reading through Part Five. Here are specific next actions you may want to record either in your task manager or in a someday/maybe list to increase the impact of the book:

❑   Remove any personal files you have stored on your employer-sponsored cloud service and transfer them to a service you pay for/own.

- ❑ Research the feasibility of automatically adjusting assignment and other dates when moving a course into a new term or semester.
- ❑ Populate and schedule key announcements for your course before starting the term/semester.
- ❑ Reconsider the deadlines that you have set for class assignments in terms of both students' needs to complete them and your needs to adequately grade them.
- ❑ Assess whether changes need to be made in your file-naming conventions or whether an entirely new scheme is needed.
- ❑ Set up favorites lists to access folders and save files faster.
- ❑ Determine whether the current cloud storage service being used is adequate for your needs.
- ❑ Audit your current backup method and ensure that it is protecting you from disasters down the road.
- ❑ Ask your information technology department about the password managers your institution offers. If you are using your own computer, research possibilities on your own and implement a password manager into your workflow.
- ❑ Visit the Thrive Online website at thriveonlineseries.com to discover other ways to boost your productivity.

CONCLUSION

*T*he *Productive Online and Offline Professor* has explored what it means to be productive; methods for facilitating communication more effectively; and how to locate, curate, and share knowledge. Additional ways of leveraging technology toward greater productivity were discussed, along with how to make as few changes as necessary within an LMS and when storing documents in the cloud.

One important means for remaining productive has been saved for last. The people whom we spend time with can have a direct effect on our emotional state, which in turn can impact our energy levels and ultimately our ability to be productive. Emdin (2017) epitomizes this sentiment:

> The kind of teacher you will become is directly related to the kind of teachers you associate with. Teaching is a profession where misery does more than just love company—it recruits, seduces, and romances it. Avoid people who are unhappy and disgruntled about the possibilities for transforming

education. They are the enemy of the spirit of the teacher. (p. 208)

As we interact with others, our moods can be influenced. Goleman (2007), an emotional intelligence researcher, recommends that we be wise about ways of infusing ourselves with positive affect by intentionally being around others who bring us greater joy:

> When we attune ourselves to someone, we can't help but feel along with them, if only subtly. We resonate so similarly that their emotions enter us— even when we don't want them to. In short, the emotions we catch have consequences. (p. 26)

Although we may not always have the luxury of choosing who we collaborate with in our work, we can select where we direct our attention. As teachers, we can choose to delight in the opportunity it is to be able to mentor and coach our students and help them discover ways of contributing to a broader learning community.

If your institution has a faculty development center, it can be an excellent resource for working through how to implement some of the tools and approaches discussed in this book. Individuals who work in faculty development can also provide a listening ear for some of the deep reflection that needs to take place whenever we consider how we are investing our time and attention in life.

One final piece of advice I will leave you with is to spend time doing absolutely nothing. Put the task list away and spend some time sitting in the sun. Notice how

One final piece of
advice I will leave
you with is to spend
time doing absolutely
nothing.

#ThriveOnline

the birds call to one another or the sound of the city where you live. We must avoid the temptation of becoming addicted to busyness, lest we miss the gifts that are in the quiet places.

As Brené Brown (2012) asserts in an interview with Lillian Cunningham,

> Crazy-busy is a great armor, it's a great way for numbing. What a lot of us do is that we stay so busy, and so out in front of our life, that the truth of how we're feeling and what we really need can't catch up with us.
>
> I see it a lot when I interview people and talk about vacation. They talk about how they are wound up and checking emails and sitting on the beach with their laptops. And their fear is: If I really stopped and let myself relax, I would crater. Because the truth is I'm exhausted, I'm disconnected from my partner, I don't feel super connected to my kids right now.
>
> It's like those moving walkways at the airport—you've got to really pay attention when you get off them, because it's disorienting. And when you're standing still, you become very acutely aware of how you feel and what's going on in your surroundings. A lot of our lives are getting away from us while we're on that walkway. (para 14)

My wish for you is that you have been able to step off the walkway a while as you read this book and consider how to have more peace in your life. Please connect with me and share what you're finding most beneficial in this quest and where you are still struggling. Tweet using the book series hashtag (#ThriveOnline) and let us know what you have found useful in exploring the practices from this book and where you still have questions. Visit the book's website (thriveonlineseries.com) for additional ways to stretch what is possible in pursuing improved productivity.

Thanks for investing the time to read *The Productive Online and Offline Professor*. As I say in introducing each *Teaching in Higher Ed* podcast, may we all have more peace in our lives so we can be even more present for our students.

APPENDIX

Productivity Tools

This appendix provides a consolidated list of the various productivity tools that are mentioned throughout the text. Additionally, alternatives are provided so you can find an option that best meets your needs. See the Thrive Online website at thriveonlineseries.com for the most up-to-date list.

AUTOMATION SERVICES

These tools let you automate steps you perform regularly, such as getting a reminder text or email when the forecast calls for rain the next day or adding a task to your to-do list whenever an email comes in that has a subject line that starts with the indicator "Todo."

- Zapier (zapier.com)
- If This, Then That (ifttt.com)
- Microsoft Flow (flow.microsoft.com)

BACKUP SERVICES

These provide places to store a duplicate of the files that are on your computer. If your computer crashes or is stolen, these services can restore your data.

- Backblaze (backblaze.com)
- Carbonite (carbonite.com)
- CrashPlan (crashplan.com)

BOOKMARK SERVICES

These services are places to save digital bookmarks such as links to interesting articles or videos you want to be able to reference later on.

- Pinboard (pinboard.in)
- Diigo (diigo.com)

CALENDAR (SEE "PLANNER" FOR ANALOG OPTIONS)

A calendar app allows you to manage all your events in one place. You can send and receive invites to events and sync your calendar across multiple devices (computer, smartphone, etc.).

- Fantastical (flexibits.com/fantastical)
- Google Calendar (google.com/calendar)
- Apple Calendar (support.apple.com/guide/calendar/welcome/mac)

- Outlook (products.office.com/en-us/outlook) (combination of functions, including calendar)

CLOUD STORAGE

Cloud storage allows you to store files on a company's server (computer) instead of or in addition to saving them on your local hard drive. This way, if your computer crashes or is stolen, you still have access to your files.

- Dropbox (dropbox.com)
- Microsoft OneDrive (onedrive.live.com/about)
- Google Drive (google.com/drive)

COLLABORATIVE WRITING APPLICATIONS

The following are ways to write in collaboration with others.

- Dropbox Paper (paper.dropbox.com)
- Google Docs (google.com/docs/about)
- Quip (quip.com)

COMMUNICATION TOOLS

The following are methods for keeping in touch with students outside of the LMS and/or a classroom.

- Remind (remind.com)
- Slack (slack.com)

EMAIL MANAGEMENT SERVICE

The following are services that sort emails using automation to leave the most important ones in your inbox, while moving the others into folders for you to look at after you have dealt with the most important messages.

- SaneBox (sanebox.com)
- Gmail Priority Inbox (support.google.com/mail/answer/186531)

LEARNING MANAGEMENT SYSTEM (LMS)

These platforms are central hubs for teaching- and learning-related activities (grading, communicating, teaching).

- Canvas (instructure.com/canvas)
- Blackboard (blackboard.com/blackboard-learn)
- D2L (d2l.com) (formerly Desire2Learn)

NOTES APPLICATION

These are applications that store notes in various formats. They can be used most effectively for the organizing portion of your GTD system.

- Evernote (evernote.com)
- Microsoft OneNote (onenote.com)
- Google Keep (keep.google.com)
- Bear (bear.app)
- Drafts (getdrafts.com)

PLANNER (PAPER)

This is an analog tool used to manage tasks, calendar items, and goals.

- Passion Planner (passionplanner.com)
- Bullet Journal (bulletjournal.com/)
- Get to Work Book (gettowork.com)
- Hipster PDA (en.wikipedia.org/wiki/Hipster_PDA)

PODCAST CATCHER

This is an app that lets you listen to a podcast on a smartphone or other portable device.

- Overcast (overcast.fm)
- Apple Podcasts (podcasts.apple.com)
- Google Podcasts (podcasts.google.com/about)
- TuneIn (tunein.com)
- Stitcher (stitcher.com)
- Spotify (spotify.com)

PROJECT MANAGEMENT SOFTWARE (FOR TEAMS)

This type of software is for helping teams capture and communicate progress toward goals and project completion.

- Microsoft Teams (products.office.com/en-us/microsoft-teams/group-chat-software)
- Asana (asana.com)
- Basecamp (basecamp.com)

REAL SIMPLE SYNDICATION (RSS) SERVICE

This service collects the most relevant information from the Internet in a single place. It is like a custom newspaper for the Internet.

- Feedly (feedly.com)
- Inoreader (inoreader.com)
- Feedbin (feedbin.com)

SCHEDULING SERVICE

This service allows students to book times to meet with you and lets you specify what time blocks you are available (e.g., during office hours). Some of them sync with your calendar, so if an appointment gets added during those times, it does not show the time as available when students are trying to schedule a meeting with you.

- Acuity Scheduling (acuityscheduling.com)
- YouCanBook.me (youcanbook.me)
- Canvas LMS Scheduler (community.canvaslms.com/docs/DOC-10719-6795261285)

SCREENCASTING APPLICATION

This is an app that allows you to record your screen to demonstrate how to do a task or to present a slide deck for your students.

- Screencast-O-Matic (screencast-o-matic.com)
- Snagit (techsmith.com/screen-capture.html)

- Studio   (instructure.com/canvas/higher-education/ platform/products/canvas-studio) (video learning platform that is integrated with Canvas LMS; has screencasting capabilities built in)

SOCIAL MEDIA

Social media are ways of cultivating a personal learning network to support lifelong learning and a personal knowledge management system.

- Twitter (twitter.com)
- Instagram (instagram.com) (bullet journaling inspiration here)
- Buffer (buffer.com) (automates the sharing of social media posts)
- MeetEdgar (meetedgar.com) (automates social media posts)

TASK MANAGER

This program keeps track of projects and tasks.

- OmniFocus (omnigroup.com/omnifocus)
- Bullet Journal method (bulletjournal.com)
- Todoist (todoist.com)

TEXT EXPANSION APPLICATION

This is a type of app that allows you to type just a few characters which then expand to expand to a longer string to automate those things you find yourself repeatedly typing (e.g., email signatures, reference letters, and reminder emails).

- TextExpander (https://textexpander.com)
- Breevy (http://www.16software.com/breevy)

VIDEOCONFERENCING SERVICE

This is a service that allows you to connect with one or more people using your computer or smartphone camera and microphone.

- Zoom (https://zoom.us)
- Skype (https://www.skype.com)

REFERENCES

Agarwal, P. (n.d.). *Retrieval practice: A powerful strategy to improve learning*. Retrieved from https://www.retrievalpractice.org/

Allen, D. (2015). *Getting things done: The art of stress-free productivity*. New York, NY: Penguin Books.

Association of American Colleges & Universities. (2014). *VALUE rubric development project*. Retrieved from https://www.aacu.org/value/rubrics

Bali, M. (2016, July 5). *Two great tools for the timezone-challenged from World Time Buddy*. Retrieved from http://www.chronicle.com/blogs/profhacker/two-great-tools-for-the-timezone-challenged-from-world-time-buddy/62432

Berg, M., & Seeber, B. K. (2016). *The slow professor: Challenging the culture of speed in the academy*. Toronto: University of Toronto Press.

Block, P. (2017). *The empowered manager: Positive political skills at work*. Hoboken, NJ: John Wiley & Sons.

Borup, J., West, R. E., & Graham, C. R. (2013). The influence of asynchronous video communication on learner social presence: A narrative analysis of four cases. *Distance Education, 34*(1), 48–63. https://doi.org/10.1080/01587919.2013.770427

Brown, B. (2012). *Daring greatly: How the courage to be vulnerable transforms the way we live, love, parent, and lead*. New York, NY: Avery.

Bruner, J. (2007). Factors motivating and inhibiting faculty in offering their courses via distance education. *Online Journal of Distance Learning Administration, 10*(2), 1–26.

Carroll, R. (n.d.). *About.* Retrieved from http://bulletjournal.com/about/

Cavender, A. (2013, November 11). *Sometimes it's the little things.* Retrieved from http://www.chronicle.com/blogs/profhacker/sometimes-its-the-little-things/53441

Cavender, A. (2016a, April 7). *Backup and development with Installatron.* Retrieved from http://www.chronicle.com/blogs/profhacker/backup-and-development-with-installatron/61974

Cavender, A. (2016b, April 28). *Tools for an effective workflow.* Retrieved from http://www.chronicle.com/blogs/profhacker/tools-for-an-effective-workflow/62086

Chickering, A. W., & Gamson, Z. F. (1999). Development and adaptations of the seven principles for good practice in undergraduate education. *TL New Directions for Teaching and Learning, 1999*(80), 75–81.

Cole, M. T., Shelley, D. J., & Swartz, L. B. (2014). Online instruction, e-learning, and student satisfaction: A three year study. *The International Review of Research in Open and Distributed Learning, 15*(6), 111–131.

Covey, S. R. (2004). *The 7 habits of highly effective people: Restoring the character ethic.* New York, NY: Free Press.

Covey, S. R. (2009). *Principle-centered leadership.* New York, NY: Rosetta Books.

Covey, S. R. (2012). *First things first.* London, UK: Simon & Schuster.

Crutchfield, R. (2018, December 27). *Meeting the needs of our students.* Retrieved from https://teachinginhighered.com/podcast/meeting-the-needs-of-our-students/

Dearnell, A. (2019, February 5). Warning: Twitter is not a toy. *Forbes.* Retrieved from https://www.forbes.com/sites/adrian.dearnell/2019/02/05/warning-twitter-is-not-a-toy/

Dini, K. (2014). *Creating flow with OmniFocus: Mastering productivity* (2nd ed.). Chicago, IL: The Dini Group.

Eisenhower, Dwight D. (1954, August 19). Dwight D. Eisenhower: Address at the Second Assembly of the World Council of Churches, Evanston, Illinois. Retrieved from https://www.globethics.net/gtl/5745992

Emdin, C. (2017). *For white folks who teach in the hood . . . and the rest of y'all too: Reality pedagogy and urban education.* Boston, MA: Beacon Press.

Felix, U. (2003). *Language learning online: Towards best practice.* Boca Raton, FL: CRC Press.

Florez, D. (2016, March 9). Why is everyone crazy for #bujo? What you need to know about "bullet journaling." *Los Angeles Times.* Retrieved from http://www.latimes.com/home/la-he-bullet-journaling-20160309-story.html

Fredrickson, C. (2015, September 15). There is no excuse for how universities treat adjuncts. *Atlantic.* Retrieved from https://www.theatlantic.com/business/archive/2015/09/higher-education-college-adjunct-professor-salary/404461/

Gawande, A. (2010). *The checklist manifesto: How to get things right.* New York, NY: Metropolitan Books.

Get to Work Book. (n.d.). Retrieved from https://www.gettoworkbook.com/

Gibbs, L. (n.d.). YouTube. Retrieved from https://www.youtube.com/user/aesopica/playlists

Goleman, D. (2007). *Social intelligence: The new science of human relationships* (Reprinted.). New York, NY: Bantam.

Grote, D. (2017, January 2). 3 Popular goal-setting techniques managers should avoid. *Harvard Business Review.* Retrieved from https://hbr.org/2017/01/3-popular-goal-setting-techniques-managers-should-avoid

Haswell, R. (1983). Minimal marking. *College English Journal, 45*(6), 600–604.

Henderson, M., & Phillips, M. (2015). Video-based feedback on student assessment: Scarily personal. *Australasian Journal of Educational Technology, 31*(1). https://doi.org/10.14742/ajet.1878

Hoffman, C. (2018, May 9). *Why you should use a password manager, and how to get started.* Retrieved from https://www

.howtogeek.com/141500/why-you-should-use-a-password-manager-and-how-to-get-started/

Houston, N. (2011, August 16). *Why checklists work*. Retrieved from http://www.chronicle.com/blogs/profhacker/why-checklists-work/35331

Houston, N. (2014, February 7). *Who do you want to be this year?* Retrieved from http://nmhouston.com/refocus-now/page/2/

Houston, N. (2015, February 5). *Practical productivity in academia*. Teaching in Higher Ed podcast. Retrieved from https://teachinginhighered.com/podcast/practical-productivity-in-academia-podcast/

Huston, T. (2012). *Teaching what you don't know*. Cambridge, MA: Harvard University Press.

Hyatt, M. (2011, April 6). *How to better control your time by designing your ideal week*. Retrieved from http://michaelhyatt.com/ideal-week.html

Inskeep, S., & Brand, M. (2010, January 5). Atul Gawande's "Checklist" for Surgery Success. In *NPR's Morning Edition*. Retrieved from http://www.npr.org/templates/story/story.php?storyId=122226184

Jarche, H. (n.d.). *Personal knowledge mastery*. Retrieved from http://jarche.com/pkm/

Jarche, H. (2014). *Why mastering personal knowledge is critical to success*. Retrieved from http://jarche.com/2014/10/why-mastering-personal-knowledge-is-critical-to-success/

Keeper Security. (2016). Keeper Security added to Internet2 NET+ program for higher education cyber theft protection. *Education Letter*, 81.

Kruse, K. (2017, April 17). *Boost your productivity with themes*. Retrieved from http://www.forbes.com/sites/kevinkruse/2017/04/17/boost-your-productivity-with-themes/

Linder, K. E. (2017, July 5). *Episode 51: My favorite time-saving strategies*. You've Got This podcast. Retrieved from https://katielinder.work/ygt51

Locke, E. A., & Latham, G. P. (2002). Building a practically useful theory of goal setting and task motivation: A 35-year odyssey. *American Psychologist, 57*(9), 705.

Mann, M. (2004, September 3). *Introducing the Hipster PDA*. Retrieved from https://www.43folders.com/2004/09/03/introducing-the-hipster-pda

Mann, M. (2007). *Inbox zero* [Video file]. Retrieved from https://www.youtube.com/watch?v=z9UjeTMb3Yk

McKee, D. (2015, March 2). *How I extract value from course evaluations*. Retrieved from http://teachbetter.co/blog/2015/03/02/learning-from-course-evaluations/

McKee, D. (2016, January 12). *Stagnation*. Retrieved from http://teachbetter.co/blog/2016/01/12/stagnation/

Meyer, K. A. (2012). The influence of online teaching on faculty productivity. *Innovative Higher Education, 37*(1), 37–52.

Michels, S.(2016). *Using Slack for teaching* [Video file]. Retrieved from https://www.youtube.com/watch?v=xfmy6EYoM_Y&feature=youtu.be

Michigan Tech. (n.d.). *Characters to avoid in directories and filenames*. Retrieved from http://www.mtu.edu/umc/services/digital/writing/characters-avoid/

Middaugh, M. F. (2001). *Understanding faculty productivity: Standards and benchmarks for colleges and universities*. San Francisco, CA: John Wiley & Sons.

Moran, B. P., & Lennington, M. (2013). *The 12 week year: Get more done in 12 weeks than others do in 12 months*. Hoboken, NJ: John Wiley & Sons.

Navarre-Cleary, M. (2014, February 25). The wrong way to teach grammar. *Atlantic*. Retrieved from https://www.theatlantic.com/education/archive/2014/02/the-wrong-way-to-teach-grammar/284014/

Newbury, P. (n.d.). Teaching + Learning Ctrs. Retrieved from https://twitter.com/polarisdotca/lists/ teaching-learning-ctrs)

Nilson, L. B. (2014). *Specifications grading: Restoring rigor, motivating students, and saving faculty time*. Sterling, VA: Stylus.

Oregon State University. (n.d.). What are good file naming conventions? Retrieved from https://webtech.training.oregonstate.edu/faq/what-are-good-file-naming-conventions

Passion Planner. (n.d.). About. Retrieved from https://passionplanner.com/

Pacheco-Vega, R. (2016, December 26). *Simplifying your document processing: The Four Trays Method.* Retrieved from http://www.raulpacheco.org/2016/12/simplifying-your-document-processing-the-four-trays-method/

Peacock, H. (2015, April 2). *An introduction to text expansion.* Retrieved from https://www.insidehighered.com/blogs/gradhacker/introduction-text-expansion

Pew Research Center. (2017, January 12). *Social media fact sheet.* Retrieved from http://www.pewinternet.org/fact-sheet/social-media/

Pham, T. (2014, June 18). *TextExpander review for on the Mac.* Retrieved from http://www.asianefficiency.com/technology/textexpander-review/

Prestopnik, M. (2015, September 8). *6 Tips to avoid frustration and increase efficiency in Blackboard.* Retrieved from https://duqedtech.wordpress.com/2015/09/08/6-tips-to-avoid-frustration-and-increase-efficiency-in-blackboard/

Reeves, D. B. (2009). *Leading change in your school: How to conquer myths, build commitment, and get results.* Alexandria, VA: ASCD.

Richardson, J., & Swan, K. (2003). *Examining social presence in online courses in relation to students' perceived learning and satisfaction.* Retrieved from https://www.ideals.illinois.edu/handle/2142/18713

Robinson, T. (2012, December 3). *The surprising connections between shame and productivity.* Retrieved from https://tararobinson.com/blog/2012/12/shame-and-productivity.html

Salter, A. (2014, May 28). *Twitter tools for summer.* Retrieved from http://www.chronicle.com/blogs/profhacker/open-thread-wednesday-twitter-tools/57137

Schmitz, M. (2013, August 6). *7 Email hacks that will save you an hour a day.* Retrieved from https://www.asianefficiency.com/email-management/7-email-hacks/

Schmitz, M. (2014, August 4). *A comprehensive video guide to TextExpander.* Retrieved from http://www.asianefficiency.com/technology/comprehensive-textexpander-guide/

Senge, P. M. (2010). *The fifth discipline: The art & practice of the learning organization*. Danvers, MA: Crown Publishing Group.

Sleeter, N. (2014, July 30). *Meaningful interaction in online courses*. Retrieved from https://www.insidehighered.com/blogs/higher-ed-beta/meaningful-interaction-online-courses

Sparks, D. (n.d.). *TextExpander snippets*. Retrieved from https://www.macsparky.com/tesnippets/

Stepper, J. (2014, January 4). *The 5 elements of working out loud*. Retrieved from https://johnstepper.wordpress.com/2014/01/04/the-5-elements-of-working-out-loud/

Stepper, J. (2016, March 2). *The 5 elements of working out loud (revisited)*. Retrieved from http://workingoutloud.com/blog/the-5-elements-of-working-out-loud-revisited

Stevens, D. D., Levi, A. J., & Walvoord, B. E. (2012). *Introduction to rubrics: An assessment tool to save grading time, convey effective feedback, and promote student learning* (2nd ed). Sterling, VA: Stylus.

Talbert, R. (2017a, January 31). *GTD for academics: Planning*. Retrieved from http://rtalbert.org/gtd-for-academics-plan/

Talbert, R. (2017b, April 21). *GTD for academics: The trimesterly review*. Retrieved from http://rtalbert.org/trimesterly-review/

Tierney, W. G. (1999). *Faculty productivity: Facts, fictions and issues*. Abingdon-on-Thames, UK: Routledge.

VanMouwerik, H. (2016, April 24). *Organize your computer with help from an archivist*. Retrieved from https://www.insidehighered.com/blogs/gradhacker/organize-your-computer-help-archivist

van Riet, H. (Producer). (2003). *Clean Sweep*. TLC.

Virtually Connecting. (2015, May 22). Retrieved from https://virtuallyconnecting.org/about/

Walker Center for Teaching and Learning, University of Tennessee at Chattanooga. (n.d.). *Seven principles for good practice in undergraduate education.* Retrieved from http://www.utc.edu/walker-center-teaching-learning/teaching-resources/7-principles.php

Watrall, E. (2009, December 17). *End of semester checklist.* Retrieved from https://www.chronicle.com/blogs/profhacker/end-of-semester-checklist/22887

Whalen, M. A. (2009). *Is time on their side? Exploring faculty time management in online and blended/hybrid higher education.* Retrieved from http://search.proquest.com.vanguard.idm.oclc.org/education/docview/304830385/abstract/6EA1C1FF571B44F4PQ/11

Zapier. (n.d.). *What is Zapier?* Retrieved from https://zapier.com/learn/getting-started-guide/what-is-zapier/

ABOUT THE AUTHOR

Bonni Stachowiak is the dean of teaching and learning and an associate professor of business and management at Vanguard University of Southern California.

As the creator and host of the *Teaching in Higher Ed* podcast, she provides a space for discussing the art and science of facilitating learning. She also explores ways to improve our productivity so we can be more present for our students and have more peace in our lives.

The podcast has welcomed such guests as James Lang, Bryan Dewsbury, Pooja Agarwal, Stephen Brookfield, Cathy Davidson, Maha Bali, Saundra McGuire, Clint Smith, Jose Bowen, Michelle Miller, Kevin Gannon, Natalie Houston, and Ken Bain. It was awarded a MERLOT Classics award (2016) and has been profiled in *The Chronicle of Higher Education*, *Inside Higher Ed*, and *EdSurge*.

Stachowiak earned a doctor of education in organizational leadership degree from Pepperdine University as well as a master of arts in organizational leadership and a bachelor's in social sciences, both from Chapman University.

Stachowiak conducts workshops and presents keynotes on how to more effectively facilitate learning. She also shares ways to use educational technology to improve teaching and approaches for providing greater agency to our students in their learning.

She is married to Dave Stachowiak, host of the *Coaching for Leaders* podcast. They have two young children, work full-time jobs, are both enthusiastic computer geeks, and are living joyfully ever after together.

INDEX

Online Learning books from Stylus Publishing

Thrive Online
A New Approach to Building Expertise and Confidence as an Online Educator
Shannon Riggs

99 Tips for Creating Simple and Sustainable Educational Videos
A Guide for Online Teachers and Flipped Classes
Karen Costa

Managing Your Professional Identity Online
A Guide for Faculty, Staff and Administrators
Kathryn E. Linder

The Business of Innovating Online
Practical Tips and Advice from E-Learning Leaders
Edited by Kathryn E. Linder

Online Learning books from Stylus Publishing

Learning to Collaborate, Collaborating to Learn
Engaging Students in the Classroom and Online
Janet Salmons

Advancing Online Teaching
Creating Equity-Based Digital Learning Environments
Kevin Kelly and Todd D. Zakrajsek

High-Impact Practices in Online Education
Research and Best Practices
Edited by Kathryn E. Linder and
Chrysanthemum Mattison Hayes

Social Presence in Online Learning
Multiple Perspectives on Practice and Research
Edited by Aimee L. Whiteside, Amy Garrett Dikkers,
and Karen Swan

Teaching and Learning books from StylusPublishing

How to Design and Teach a Hybrid Course
Achieving Student-Centered Learning through Blended Classroom, Online and Experiential Activities
Jay Caulfield

Discussion-Based Online Teaching To Enhance Student Learning
Theory Practice and Assessment
Tisha Bender

eService-Learning
Creating Experiential Learning and Civic Engagement Through Online and Hybrid Courses
Edited by Jean R. Strait and Katherine Nordyke

Creating Wicked Students
Designing Courses for a Complex World
Paul Hanstedt

Teaching and Learning books from Stylus Publishing

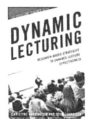

Dynamic Lecturing
Research-Based Strategies to Enhance Lecture Effectiveness
Christine Harrington and Todd Zakrajsek
Foreword by José Antonio Bowen

Creating Engaging Discussions
Strategies for "Avoiding Crickets" in Any Size Classroom and Online
Jennifer H. Herman and Linda B. Nilson
Foreword by Stephen D. Brookfield

Hitting Pause
65 Lecture Breaks to Refresh and Reinforce Learning
Gail Taylor Rice
Foreword by Kevin Barry

Connected Teaching
Relationships, Power, and Mattering in Higher Education
Harriet L. Schwartz
Foreword by Laurent A. Daloz

Jump-Start Your Online Classroom

Mastering Five Challenges in Five Days

David S. Stein and Constance E. Wanstreet

Jump-Start Your Online Classroom prepares a first-time online instructor to successfully manage the first few weeks of a course, including activities to help instructors plan, manage, and facilitate online instruction and provides resources helpful during the beginning weeks of class. Each chapter is developed around the immediate challenges instructors face when teaching online. The authors address everyday problems and suggest solutions informed by their extensive research and experience.

The book is based on the authors' design and facilitation model that identifies five elements comprising an online learning environment: digital tools, participants, social practices, learning community, and outcomes. The book shows how each of those aspects influences instructional practices and interacts to create an environment for a meaningful online educational experience.

22883 Quicksilver Drive
Sterling, VA 20166-2019

Subscribe to our email alerts: www.Styluspub.com

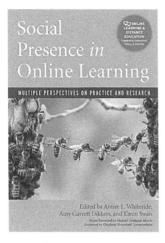

Edited by Aimee L. Whiteside,
Amy Garrett Dikkers, and Karen Swan
Series Foreword by Michael Grahame Moore
Foreword by Charlotte Nirmalani Gunawardena

Social Presence in Online Learning

Multiple Perspectives on Practice and Research

Edited by Aimee L. Whiteside, Amy Garrett Dikkers, and Karen Swan

Foreword by Charlotte Nirmalani Gunawardena

Series Foreword by Michael Grahame Moore

"*Social Presence in Online Learning* is of great importance to those in the field of online and blended learning. The insights provided in this book make it clear that social presence represents an essential element of any collaborative learning experience—online and otherwise. The comprehensive treatment of the social presence construct makes this book a key resource for those interested in online learning." —*D. Randy Garrison*, Professor Emeritus, University of Calgary

Understanding social presence—with its critical connections to community-building, retention, and learning outcomes—allows faculty and instructional designers to better support and engage students. This volume addresses the evolution of social presence with three distinct perspectives, outlines the relevant research, and focuses on practical strategies that can immediately impact the teaching and learning experience.

(Continues on preceding page)

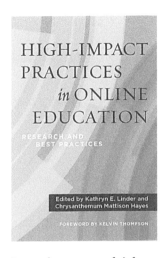

High-Impact Practices in Online Education

Research and Best Practices

Kathryn E. Linder and Chrysanthemum Mattison Hayes

Foreword by Kelvin Thompson

"High-Impact Practices in Online Education asks the right questions about online teaching and learning. This collection offers grounded, practical suggestions for evolving online pedagogy toward a purposeful form of teaching that offers possibilities beyond anything we've done until now."—**Matthew Reed**, *Vice President for Learning - Brookdale Community College*

The Blended Course Design Workbook

A Practical Guide

Kathryn E. Linder

"The Blended Course Design Workbook brings together the best practices in online learning and residential teaching in a single concise volume and provides a wealth of resources, checklists, and step-by-step instructions essential for the development and teaching of cutting-edge college courses."—**Joshua Kim**, *Director of Digital Learning Initiatives - Dartmouth Center for the Advancement of Learning (DCAL)*

(Continues on preceding page)

Also available from Stylus

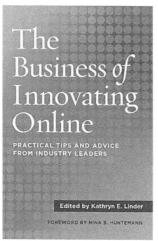

The Business of Innovating Online

Practical Tips and Advice From Industry Leaders

Edited by Kathryn E. Linder

Foreword by Nina Huntemann

The Business of Innovating Online provides both novice and experienced online education administrators with a comprehensive overview of a range of online innovations, how they came to be created, the components that led to their success, and concrete steps that they can take to create a more innovative culture for their own e-learning organization.

(Continues on preceding page)